# How To Start Your Own Business

The Success Guide to Understand Complex Concepts, Secure Start-Up Funds, and Make Your Entrepreneurial Dream a Reality with Zero Experience

Waldo's Publishing Company

WALDO'S PUBLISHING
EST.
2024
COMPANY

**If you're embarking on the thrilling journey of entrepreneurship, pairing "How to Start Your Own Business: Workbook" with this companion book is an essential step towards success.**

This workbook isn't just a guide; it's a hands-on toolkit packed with practical exercises, detailed checklists, and expert advice. Each section is designed to help you build a solid foundation for your business, from concept to launch and beyond. By the end of this workbook, you'll have a clear roadmap to success and the confidence to navigate the challenges of entrepreneurship.

This workbook includes:

- Exercises to determine the right path for Securing Start-Up Capital

- Exercises to help you determine the best structure fit for your business.

- Start-up Budget Template.

- Creative exercises to define your brand identity.

- And Much More!

**GET YOUR COPY HERE!**

# Contents

# Introduction

Every great journey begins with a single step, even the journey of transforming a simple idea into a thriving business. Think of the endless possibilities of being your own boss and making your mark in the world. It's about making money and bringing something you believe to life. This journey is filled with moments of triumph, creativity, and the pure joy of building something from the ground up. That's the entrepreneurial dream, and it's more achievable than you might think.

The purpose of this book is simple: to strip away the mystery of starting your own business and lay down a clear, practical path for you to follow. This isn't just about lofty ideas or theoretical success; it's a hands-on guide filled with actionable advice, step-by-step strategies, and real-world examples to get you from dreaming to doing.

This book was created with you in mind, the average person who dreams big but might feel overwhelmed by the nitty-gritty details or intimidated by the hurdles ahead. Whether it's navigating complex concepts, making sense of the best structure for your business, finding the funds to get started, or figuring out your marketing strategy, I've got you covered. I understand that the idea of starting a business can feel like a giant leap, especially if you're stepping into unknown territory. That's exactly why I've broken everything down into understandable steps.

What sets this book apart is its foundation on real-life success stories and case studies. These aren't just tales of triumph but lessons packed with practical insights. You'll find actionable steps, checklists, and templates you can directly apply to your entrepreneurial journey. It's one thing to read about success; it's another to understand the steps taken to get there and see how you can do the same.

Having fears and facing challenges is normal when venturing into the business world. Fear of failure, concerns about funding, and feeling like you're not quite an expert are common. But let me tell you, every successful entrepreneur has overcome these same fears. This book is here to be your guide, encouragement, and tool to get through these hurdles.

As we dive into this book, you'll find it divided into practical parts, each designed to take you closer to your goal. From concept to launch, we'll cover everything you need to know and do. Remember, achieving success is a journey that requires dedication, hard work, and a willingness to learn and adapt. Each chapter includes key takeaways and action items to ensure you're actively moving toward making your dream a reality.

So, are you ready to take that first step? Approach this book with an open mind and a readiness to apply its lessons. Your entrepreneurial journey is about to get much clearer, and I'm here to guide you through it.

# Chapter One

# Transforming Your Vision into a Plan

In the journey of starting a business, the first steps are often the most crucial, laying the groundwork for future success. Every successful business begins not with a grand opening or a groundbreaking product launch but with a vision. A clear, compelling picture of the future that the business seeks to create. This vision serves as the map that guides decisions, actions, and the allocation of resources. Without such a vision, businesses may find themselves adrift, subject to the whims of the market or the pressures of competition. Hence, the vision infuses a business with purpose, steers its direction, and opens up a realm of possibilities.

## Defining Your Business Vision

The foundation of any lasting business starts with grasping the "why," the core purpose that drives its creation. This foundational question transcends profit margins and market share, delving into the personal and professional motivations that fuel the entrepreneurial spirit. It's about uncovering the passion that drives you, the problems you aim to solve, and the impact you wish to have on the world. Consider the case of a local organic bakery. Its "why" might not just be to sell bread but also to foster community health, support sustainable agriculture, or even revive traditional baking techniques. This deeper purpose serves as the basis for all other business decisions, ensuring that each step taken is aligned with the core reason for the business's existence.

A business driven by a clear purpose uniquely inspires its founders, employees, customers, and the wider community, fostering a sense of unity and shared goals among all stakeholders. This purpose is a magnetic force, attracting individuals who share or support the business's core values and vision. It shapes the creation of products, the approach to marketing, and how we connect with customers, crafting a narrative that resonates and deeply connects with everyone associated with the business. Moreover, a purpose-driven approach fosters a strong organizational culture that empowers employees and encourages innovation, adaptability, and resilience.

Visualization, creating a vivid mental image of a desired future state, is a crucial tool in the entrepreneur's arsenal. It involves more than daydreaming about success; it's an exercise in precision, crafting a detailed picture of what success looks like for your business. Perhaps it's envisioning the bustling environment of your dream coffee shop, the grateful smiles of satisfied clients, or the global reach of your innovative app. This mental imagery serves as a starting point, guiding the path forward and keeping motivation alive through the inevitable ups and downs of business growth.

A vision statement crystallizes your business's ultimate aspirations into a concise, powerful declaration. It encapsulates what you aim to achieve long-term, constantly reminding you of your business's purpose and direction. Crafting this statement requires reflection and foresight, then essentializing your grand ambitions to a few powerful lines. It's about capturing the heart of what you aim to achieve and articulating it concisely. Imagine a tech start-up with the goal of making education universally accessible. Their vision statement might be, "To unlock free, top-tier educational resources for everyone worldwide." This sets a clear, ambitious target and energizes everyone involved to turn that dream into reality. Such a statement communicates the scope and scale of the ambition and inspires action and commitment.

The true test of a vision lies in its translation into action. This alignment ensures that every decision made moves the business closer to its envisioned future. It requires a methodical approach, setting specific, measurable goals that serve as milestones on the journey toward realizing the vision. Moreover, it demands flexibility and the willingness to adapt strategies and tactics in response to feedback and changing circumstances, all while keeping the overarching vision in focus.

In pursuing a business vision, entrepreneurs embark on a journey fraught with challenges, uncertainties, and moments of doubt. Yet, this vision provides clarity amidst chaos, motivation amidst adversity, and direction amidst distraction. By defining and refining your vision, you lay the foundation for your business that is not only successful but also meaningful, impactful, and enduring.

> **Action Step:** Determine your why, your purpose, and what you want your business to become. Develop a few statements to capture this vision.

## Crafting Your Mission Statement

A mission statement is more than a sentence on a website; it's the heartbeat of a business, guiding every decision, every product, and every customer interaction. It articulates the present operations and the immediate intentions, capturing the essence of a business's goals and how it intends to achieve them. This declaration is pivotal, guiding internal strategies and actions and communicating to the external world what the business stands for, its values, and its unique proposition.

A powerful mission statement is made up of several core elements, each serving a distinct purpose. It must be clear at its core, clearly expressing the business's intentions. It should be concise, eliminating unnecessary language to reveal the essence of the business's purpose. Yet, it must be compelling, with the power to inspire those within the company and its customers. Including tangible objectives gives it power, making the mission actionable rather than aspirational. Finally, it must resonate with the values of its audience, aligning the business's goals with those of its stakeholders.

Shaping such a statement begins with reflection, a deep dive into the core of the business to unearth the values and principles that form its foundation. From this base of understanding, the process of crafting the mission statement can begin. Start with a broad description of what the business does, focusing on the impact it seeks to have rather than the mechanics of its operations. Next, refine this description, honing in on the unique approach or values that differentiate the business. Incorporate specific, achievable objectives, ensuring these aims are grounded in reality but also stretch the business to reach higher. Throughout this process, the language used should be vivid and powerful, painting a picture of the business's purpose and how it engages with the world.

## Examples of Successful Mission Statements

"Build the best product, cause no unnecessary harm, use business to inspire and implement solutions to the environmental crisis." – Patagonia, an outdoor apparel company

This statement is a masterclass in clarity and conciseness, immediately conveying what the company does and how it does it. But more than that, it's compelling, positioning the business not just as a seller of goods but as a force for environmental advocacy. It's specific, with a commitment to quality and sustainability, and it's value-aligned, resonating with the concerns and priorities of its eco-conscious customers.

"Spread ideas." – TED, a nonprofit devoted to spreading ideas

This statement is simple yet profound; it captures the essence of the organization's intent and method. It's a strong call to action, inviting participation and engagement from all who interact with it. It underscores the power of ideas to change attitudes, lives, and, ultimately, the world.

These examples underscore the transformative potential of a well-conceived mission statement. Beyond a marketing tool, it's a standard, guiding the business through the complexities of its environment and growth challenges. It's a standard for decision-making, a benchmark against which actions can be measured, and a banner under which employees and customers alike can rally.

The creation of a mission statement is not the end but the beginning. It requires regular revisitation and, as necessary, revision. The business landscape is dynamic, and as a business evolves, its mission may also need to adapt to reflect new goals, markets, or challenges. Yet, through all these changes, the mission statement remains a constant reminder of the business's core purpose and its commitment to its values.

In sum, your mission statement needs to be a compact but powerful expression of your business's purpose, encapsulating the company's ambitions, values, and essence in a few carefully chosen words. Creating your mission statement involves a thoughtful process of refining your ideas. It demands deep introspection, careful planning, and a thorough grasp of both your business's essence and the needs of those it serves. When done right, it becomes an invaluable asset, guiding the business's strategy, operations, and culture and communicating its purpose and promise to the world.

> **Action Step:** Create a few mission statements based on your vision. At this step, these do not need to be perfect, as they may change as you start your due diligence.

## Market Research: Your Customers & Competitors

When launching a business, understanding the complexities of your operational environment is not merely beneficial; it's imperative. Market research, the collection, documentation, and examination of information concerning the marketing of goods and services, serves as your navigating tool through the intricate and competitive terrain of the business environment. This process begins with identifying who your customers are and extends to understanding your competitors, thereby ensuring that your business not only enters the market but thrives within it.

At its core, market research involves a variety of methodologies, each tailored to uncover specific angles of the market landscape. Surveys and interviews are recourse for gauging your target audience's preferences and needs. Market analysis helps evaluate the overall market size, growth trends, and dynamics, while competitor analysis sheds light on your rivals' strategies, strengths, and weaknesses in the marketplace. Together, these methodologies provide a comprehensive understanding of where your business fits within the market landscape. Market research can be achieved through various tools, including social media groups, AI research, online platforms, and professional consultants. Deciding which tool or tools to employ depends on your budget and time constraints, as they offer varying levels of detail and speed of results.

A careful examination of market research data reveals opportunities within the market, areas where customer needs are not fully met, and segments that are overlooked. This process is similar to finding missing pieces in a puzzle, each one representing a chance to introduce your unique value proposition. For instance, if research reveals a consistent demand for environmentally friendly packaging among consumers in your target market, yet few providers meet this need, a significant gap and opportunity become clear. Your business could then position itself to fill this void, addressing a specific, unmet demand.

Identifying your ideal customer requires precision. It's about pinpointing potential customers of your product or service and those actively seeking it. This involves market segmentation, dividing potential customers based on demographics, psychographics, geographic location, and behaviors to determine your target segment. The aim is to create a detailed profile of your ideal customer, capturing their preferences, motivations, and behaviors. This insight allows for customizing your offerings and marketing strategies, ensuring they connect with the most receptive audience.

Validating your business idea is a pivotal step in the entrepreneurial process. It involves testing your product or service with your target audience to gauge its potential for market demand. This might be a prototype, a minimum viable product, or a pilot service offered to a select group of potential customers for feedback. The insights from this process are invaluable, providing a direct window into the minds of your potential customers. They enable you to refine your offering, adjusting features, pricing, or positioning to meet market demand better.

Learning from the competition is about strategic differentiation. By analyzing the successes and failures of your competitors, you gain insights into what resonates with your target audience and where there may be gaps in the market. This knowledge enables you to carve out a unique niche for your business, one that leverages your strengths and capitalizes on the unaddressed needs of your target audience. You need to find the balance between fitting within your market and standing apart from it, ensuring your business attracts attention for the right reasons.

Differentiating your business in the eyes of your target audience is both an art and a science. It requires a keen understanding of what sets your business apart, such as superior quality, innovative features, exceptional service, or a unique brand story. This differentiation must be communicated clearly and compellingly across all customer touchpoints, from your website and social media channels to your packaging and customer service. The goal is to embed your unique value proposition in the minds of your target audience, ensuring that when they think of your product or service category, your business stands out as the preferred choice.

In conclusion, market research is the cornerstone of successful businesses. It provides the insights necessary to understand your customers and competitors, identify market gaps, validate your business idea, and strategically differentiate your business. By approaching this process with diligence, curiosity, and a commitment to learning, you set the foundation for a business that makes a lasting impact within the market.

> **Action Step:** Choose the best market research tool or tools for you and conduct your market research.
>
> **Action Step:** From your market research determine your target audience, competitors, and validity of your business idea.

## Setting Achievable Goals: Your Roadmap to Success

In the process of launching a business, establishing clear goals is vital. It is the skeleton that holds the business together, ensuring that every action taken and resource utilized serves a well-defined journey toward success. Consider setting goals as drawing a map before embarking on a sea voyage. Skipping this step can lead to drifting aimlessly, at the mercy of unpredictable elements. Goals help visualize the future not as random occurrences but as deliberate steps toward achievement. This turns vague dreams into concrete targets, making the ambitious achievable.

The core of successful goal setting is rooted in following key principles. These principles serve as the support structure for your goals, ensuring they provide a reliable path to success. The **SMART** framework is key here, providing a blueprint for crafting ambitious and achievable goals.

- **S**pecific goals clarify exactly what you aim to accomplish, removing any uncertainty.

- **M**easurable goals introduce tangible benchmarks for tracking progress.

- **A**chievable goals ensure your targets are within reach, pushing the limits of what's possible while remaining realistic.

- **R**elevant goals tie directly into your business's overall mission, ensuring every effort contributes to your ultimate objectives.

- **T**ime-bound goals set deadlines, creating a sense of urgency and focus.

The standard provided by this framework transforms lofty aspirations into actionable, down-to-earth plans.

The interplay between short-term and long-term goals is essential for business strategy. Short-term goals provide immediate, achievable targets that act as stepping stones to more significant, long-term objectives. They keep the business momentum going, allowing for quick wins that boost morale and offer chances for adjustments. Meanwhile, long-term goals serve as the overarching vision, directing the business's journey through operational challenges. Achieving a balance between these ensures that daily efforts support broader ambitions, harmonizing immediate actions with the ultimate vision of success. This balance is crucial, aligning the day-to-day progress with the end goals and ensuring a coherent path to success.

The journey toward goal achievement is punctuated by milestones, each marking a step closer to the envisioned future. Tracking and measuring progress against these milestones is crucial, indicating the business's forward movement. Key performance indicators (KPIs) take center stage in this journey, acting as quantifiable benchmarks that shine a light on the effectiveness of strategies and the smoothness of operations. These metrics, whether financial indicators like revenue growth and profit margins or operational metrics such as customer acquisition rates and product development timelines, consistently offer a transparent perspective on the business's progress toward its goals. This clarity supports informed decision-making and strategic pivots.

Flexibility in goal setting is essential, reflecting a business's ability to adapt in a dynamic market. Instead of viewing goals as rigid markers, treat them as flexible guideposts that can be adjusted in response to feedback, market trends, or internal shifts. This adaptability is a strength, empowering the business to overcome obstacles and capitalize on new opportunities. Recognizing that the path to success is rarely straight allows for a more strategic approach and an openness to change.

Within this framework, goal setting transitions from a singular task to a continuous aspect of business operations. It requires regular assessment of strategies to monitor progress, celebrate achievements, and set new goals. This iterative process keeps the business on track, enabling agile adjustments to leverage opportunities and navigate challenges. It fosters a culture of ongoing advancement, with each achieved goal paving the way for the next, driving the business toward continuous growth, innovation, and success.

In sum, goals are the backbone of any successful business, transcending mere aspirations to become the foundation of success. They steer the business amidst market uncertainties toward achieving its vision. Businesses can navigate toward sustainable growth by strategically setting SMART goals, balancing immediate and future objectives, and closely monitoring progress.

> **Action Step:** Using the SMART method, determine a few long-term and short-term goals for your business.

## The Art of Business Naming: Crafting an Identity

In the competitive business world, a name is more than a simple identifier; it encapsulates a company's values, spirit, and goals. It marks the initial interaction with the market, acting as a magnet that draws attention, encourages recognition, and establishes a fundamental connection with the intended audience. Therefore, choosing a business name goes beyond ordinary branding efforts; it becomes a crucial strategic decision with wide-reaching effects. The right name can captivate, set you apart, and foster affinity, whereas the wrong choice might lead to confusion, detachment, or invisibility amidst the market's hustle and bustle.

The journey to a compelling business name typically starts with a vibrant brainstorming session, where creativity flows without restraint. Word association is an effective technique that encourages the sharing of ideas linked to the business's core offerings, values, or objectives. This process reveals various potential names, each reflecting the business's essence and vision. By also incorporating creative thinking exercises, such as imagining the business as a character or a unique piece of art, these brainstorming sessions promote innovative thinking. This approach transforms abstract concepts into concrete naming options, generating diverse names that capture different facets of the business's identity.

Navigating the legal landscape of business naming introduces complexity to this creative process. It begins with a detailed trademark search to ensure your chosen name doesn't infringe on existing trademarks, a step that safeguards against legal issues and confirms the name's uniqueness. Equally important is checking the availability of domain names, which is crucial in today's digital world for building a strong online presence. Securing a domain that matches the business name reinforces brand identity and improves online visibility and accessibility. These legal steps, essential and rooted in practicality, guarantee that your chosen name is legally sound and market-ready. There are several online tools to assist in domain availability and trademarks.

Selecting the perfect business name concludes in the testing phase, where your top choices are evaluated by the public. Sharing potential names with your target market through surveys, focus groups, or social media polls provides essential feedback on the names' resonance, memorability, and alignment with your business identity. This process, conducted from your future customers' perspectives, refines your options. The chosen name emerges from this phase not merely as a label but as a true representation of your business's essence and values, fostering a deep connection with your target market.

Crafting a business name is a creative, strategic, and legal endeavor requiring a well-rounded approach that merges imagination with practicality. This vital process involves expansive thinking, meticulous attention, and a keen grasp of the business's core identity and position in the market. The selected name stands as the brand's foundation, serving as a critical component for market introduction, customer connection, and the business's overall success.

> **Action Step:** Brainstorm potential names, verify their availability, and receive customer input. Repeat until you have landed on your company's name.

## The Business Model Canvas: A Blueprint for Success

Within the framework of strategic planning and business development, the Business Model Canvas stands out as a critical tool. This structured representation provides a clear picture of a company's operational framework, covering its value proposition, infrastructure, customer base, and financials. The canvas presents an integrated view of a business's key functions and their connections, simplifying complex planning elements. Its true power stems from its adaptability, acting as a living tool that grows and changes with the business.

The canvas is broken out into nine key elements, each crucial to your business's overall structure. At the core of this model is the value proposition, the distinct advantage your business presents to its customers, setting it apart from the competition. This proposition is the cornerstone of the Business Model Canvas, influencing every other element with its importance. Identifying your target market within the customer segments section is essential, as well as organizing potential customers based on common characteristics and needs. This strategic grouping ensures that your value proposition is aligned to effectively meet each segment's demands.

Channels represent the routes through which your business communicates its value proposition to customer segments. Identifying and utilizing the most effective and preferred ways to interact and transact with your target audience is essential. The customer relationships section explores the depth of interactions between the business and its customers, outlining strategies to attract, retain, and increase customer satisfaction and loyalty. Following this, the section on revenue streams highlights the diverse ways a business generates income from its customer segments. It details the different ways the business's value is transformed into financial gain.

Turning to the other side of the canvas, we examine the business's essential assets and key resources. The key resources include physical assets, intellectual property, human talent, and financial resources, all of which are vital for successful operation and value delivery. We then cover key activities and the critical tasks necessary to fulfill the value proposition, engage customers, and ensure smooth operations. Following this, we note key partnerships, emphasizing the importance of a supportive network of suppliers and collaborators for business success and the role of teamwork in the business model. Lastly, we address the cost structure, offering insight into the business's primary expenses and financial management strategies to optimize resource allocation and value generation.

Navigating the process of completing your own Business Model Canvas begins with a deep dive into each component, treating them not as isolated elements but as interconnected gears in a larger machine. Mapping out the canvas encourages a meticulous examination of every business component, prompting questions, provoking thought, and illuminating the relationships between different parts of the business model. It requires an inner look at the business's internal workings and an outward look, considering the market, competition, and the broader playing field in which the business operates.

Completing the Business Model Canvas is not a one-time task but a continuous journey that evolves alongside your business. Initially, you'll make educated guesses to fill out various sections of the canvas. Yet, as your business grows, these initial assumptions will be tested through real-world experiences, feedback from the market, and operational performance data. This process of receiving and integrating feedback is crucial, as it forms a loop that informs necessary adjustments to your business model. Such a tool keeps your business adaptable, ensuring it remains aligned with market demands and consistently aligned with its long-term goals.

The Business Model Canvas shines as a vital tool for simplification and organization, turning the complex task of business planning into a clearer process. The canvas becomes an essential blueprint for success. This tool is where the journey of your entrepreneurial dream takes shape and becomes a reality.

**Action Step:** Craft your Unique Value Proposition (UVP). Reflect on the core problem your business solves and how it does so uniquely. Draft a single sentence encapsulating this, ensuring it's specific, clear, and compelling.

**Action Step:** Complete your Business Model Canvas.

# Chapter Two

# Writing Your Business Plan: Legal and Financial Foundations

In the entrepreneurship journey, a business plan is your guide, showing the way among uncertainties. It serves as a strategic roadmap, steering your start-up idea toward success. Far from just a formality, a business plan is a crucial tool that embeds your venture in practicality, forward-thinking, and flexibility. It's essential for obtaining funding and acts as a blueprint that provides clear guidance and evolves as your business expands and adapts.

Consider the careful planning that goes into launching a new restaurant. Before the kitchen springs to life or a single customer is welcomed, every aspect is thoughtfully planned, from the menu's design to the kitchen's layout, the selection of suppliers, and the customer service protocols. This meticulous preparation embodies the purpose of a business plan: forecasting, planning, and outlining the journey from an idea to a thriving business. It caters to a diverse group, including investors, lenders, and your own team, all of whom seek confidence that your vision is built on a solid, strategic foundation.

# Business Plans Demystified: A Step-by-Step Guide

At its core, a business plan comprises several key components, each unfolding a different component of the business vision and strategy. The **executive summary** acts as the gateway, offering a snapshot of the business's essence and aspiration and enticing readers to delve deeper. **Market analysis** lays the groundwork, detailing the marketplace terrain, the target audience's needs, and the competitive landscape. **Financial projections** offer the numerical heartbeat of the plan, quantifying the business's potential for profitability and growth.

One size does not fit all when it comes to business plans. The lens through which an investor views your plan differs vastly from that of a bank or even your internal team. Investors might look for growth potential and scalability, and banks look for stability and risk mitigation while your team seeks clarity on vision and operational structure. Tailoring your plan means emphasizing the aspects most relevant to each audience, ensuring the message resonates, and the purpose aligns with their interests and expectations.

As previously discussed in Chapter 1, conducting a thorough market analysis is crucial. It acts as your guide, rooting your business strategy in real market demands and trends. Including your **target market**, the insights gained from **analyzing customer needs**, and a **competitive analysis** in your business plan is vital. These components, introduced and determined earlier, are essential for crafting an informed and strategically positioned plan to meet market realities.

Financial planning within a business plan lays the foundation for fiscal health and sustainability. Starting with **budgeting**, this process outlines the operational and capital expenditures necessary to launch and sustain the business. **Revenue forecasting** extends the financial vision into the future, predicting income streams and growth trajectories. **Cash flow analysis** keeps the business's pulse, tracking the ebb and flow of funds in and out, ensuring liquidity and operational stability. We will dive deeper into financial specifics later in this chapter.

Navigating the complexities of financial forecasting and budgeting can be challenging, especially if this isn't your area of expertise. Seeking advice from financial experts can enhance your plan, reducing errors and ensuring a solid, dependable strategy for your business's fiscal health.

A business plan, in essence, is more than the sum of its parts. It's a coherent narrative combining the vision, strategy, market understanding, and financial projections into a compelling story of potential success. Templates serve as the base for this story, offering structure and guidance, yet your business's unique details fill the pages with life. Beware the pitfalls of over-ambition without evidence or vagueness that leaves more questions than answers. Aim for clarity, precision, and realism, grounding your aspirations in the solid bedrock of research, strategy, and planning.

## Business Plan Checklist

- Executive Summary: Clear, compelling, and concise

- Market Analysis: Detailed, data-supported, and insightful

- Financial Projections: Realistic, comprehensive, and clear

- Strategy and Implementation: Specific, actionable, and adaptable

- Appendices and Supporting Documents: Relevant, organized, and accessible

This checklist is your final review, ensuring that every aspect of your plan is refined, every detail is substantiated, and your overall narrative is persuasive. It's like the last check before launch, making sure everything is in order, your strategy is solid, and you're fully prepared to embark on your business journey.

**Action Step:** Begin filling out your business plan template by using your Business Model Canvas as a foundational guide. Incorporate insights from your market analysis outlined in Chapter 1. As you work through this chapter, revisit your financial sections to integrate the outcomes of the action steps detailed later, ensuring a comprehensive and cohesive plan.

# Understanding Business Structures: Choosing the Right One for You

Choosing the right business structure is crucial in starting your venture. This decision significantly impacts how you operate, your personal liability, tax requirements, and your ability to expand. Initially, entrepreneurs face several options: sole proprietorship, partnership, corporation, etc., each offering unique advantages and challenges.

## Overview of Business Structures

**Sole Proprietorship:** A sole proprietorship is optimal for self-employed individuals like freelancers or consultants. It requires minimal formalities beyond potential local licensing, making starting easy. However, this ease comes at the cost of the owner's unlimited legal and financial responsibility. This means the owner's personal and business finances are intertwined, which can hinder securing business credit or loans. For tax purposes, the business's income is considered the owner's personal income, simplifying tax filings but merging personal and business financial matters.

**General Partnership:** Similar to a sole proprietorship, a general partnership allows two or more owners to collaborate. While formal registration may not be required, local licenses could be necessary. In this structure, all partners share legal and financial responsibilities equally. This means that each partner can be held liable for the actions or negligence of the others. Profits and losses are distributed evenly among the partners and reported on each partner's tax returns, blending business and personal financial matters.

**Limited Partnership (LP):** This structure requires state registration and encompasses two distinct partner roles: general and limited. The general partner manages the business's daily operations and bears full legal and financial responsibility, with their share of the profits being taxed on personal taxes. The limited partner, often an investor, plays a less active role and enjoys limited liability, meaning they are not personally responsible for business debts or legal issues, provided they do not partake in management activities. This arrangement typically results in lower personal taxation for the limited partner than the general partner.

**Limited Liability Company (LLC):** LLCs safeguard owners' (members') personal assets against business debts and liabilities. Establishing an LLC requires filing with the state annually. Membership can include an unlimited number of individuals, all of whom must be declared at the time of filing. However, should a member decide to leave, the LLC may face dissolution and require re-registration. While profits and losses pass through to members' personal tax returns, positioning them as self-employed, an election can be submitted during the registration process for the LLC to be taxed as a corporation, offering flexibility in tax management.

**S Corporation (S Corp):** S Corps offer similar personal asset protections to LLCs, safeguarding shareholders' personal assets from business liabilities. However, shareholders are accountable for the company's financial outcomes. This business structure transforms your venture into a corporation but imposes certain ownership restrictions. Notably, there is a cap of 100 shareholders, and all shareholders must be individuals or certain trusts. Corporate entities cannot hold shares, potentially complicating efforts to raise start-up capital. Additionally, shareholders must be U.S. resident aliens. Taxation for S Corps operates on a pass-through basis, meaning profits and losses are reported on the shareholders' personal tax returns, avoiding double taxation. Shareholders must draw a "reasonable compensation" salary, subject to Social Security and Medicare taxes, which ensures taxation occurs only once. Establishing an S Corp involves state registration and adherence to more stringent formalities compared to other structures, including providing detailed business information during the annual renewal process, with specific requirements varying by state.

**C Corporation (C Corp):** C Corps are recognized internationally, offering the flexibility to issue stock options as a means to secure start-up funding without restrictions related to U.S. residency or corporate entity status. This structure distinctly separates an owner's personal liabilities from those of the business. C Corps are independently taxable entities, adhering to corporate tax laws, which leads to double taxation, firstly at the corporate level and secondly at the individual level when shareholders receive dividends or salaries. Registration at the state level is mandatory, necessitating comprehensive documentation, including the appointment of board members, recording of board meeting minutes, and more. Although this may seem daunting, a single individual can occupy all required board positions. The specifics regarding documentation and filing can vary from state to state.

## Factors to Consider

When deciding on the right business structure, three key considerations are crucial: liability, taxes, and scalability. The fear of personal financial risk often pushes entrepreneurs away from sole proprietorships toward structures that offer better protection, like LLCs or corporations. Tax implications vary significantly by structure and location and can directly impact your profitability. Furthermore, choosing a structure that supports growth without adding undue complexity or cost is important for expansion.

## Process of Establishment

Establishing your business begins with selecting a unique name and registering with the relevant authorities. Complexity varies by the chosen business structure and location. This process includes interactions with various agencies, from local licensing offices to national tax authorities, each vital for business validation. Registering your business involves understanding and complying with various rules that differ by location. Each area has its own requirements for what your business name can be, what documents you need to file, and what fees you must pay. Success in this process requires a thorough understanding of legal requirements and forward planning to ensure your business's name and structure support future growth without restrictions.

## Local Regulations and Compliance

After setting up your business, your chosen structure significantly influences your interaction with local laws and compliance obligations. This includes the necessity for annual filings, tax declarations, and operational disclosures, among others, aligning your business operations with the surrounding legal and regulatory environment. Failing to adhere to these requirements can result in penalties, missed opportunities, or even the business being shut down in severe situations.

## Avoiding Common Pitfalls

Selection and establishment of your business structure come with challenges, including the risk of selecting an unsuitable structure or overlooking important local regulations. It's essential for entrepreneurs to proceed with caution, equipped with the right knowledge, strategic insights, and a clear understanding of their business's current needs and future goals. Various resources are available to aid in this process, such as consulting with tax professionals or using an online service. Leveraging these resources is highly recommended to guarantee adherence to legal requirements and to choose the business structure that best suits your venture.

> **Action Step:** Determine the right structure for your business.

## Financial Planning for Start-Ups: Budgets, Forecasts, and More

Building the financial foundation of a start-up is like drawing a detailed map, where every line has a purpose, contributing to the overall strength and growth. Financial planning is not just one of the steps in starting a business; it's the core support that keeps it alive through market ups and downs. This essential stage in developing a start-up requires detailed focus, an understanding of economic influences, and foresight to anticipate financial challenges. This section will explore the key concepts of financial planning and the foundation for your business planning. The concepts introduced here will be further explored and expanded upon in a later chapter dedicated to Financial Mastery.

Creating a realistic budget is a balance of ambition and practicality. Entrepreneurs must forecast initial and ongoing costs, as well as unforeseen expenses. This includes start-up costs such as licenses, equipment, marketing, website setup, and recurring costs like rent, utilities, wages, and supplies, which may grow with your business. Importantly, a contingency fund should be integrated into your budget to safeguard against unexpected financial challenges, ensuring your start-up remains stable.

### Start-Up Budget Checklist:

- Start-up Costs: This includes any one-time costs such as purchasing licenses, equipment, and making deposits. Additionally, you'll encounter recurring expenses like rent, phone services, payroll, and more.

- Fixed Costs (Overhead): These are expenses incurred on a monthly basis, such as payroll, rent, and insurance, among others.

- Variable Costs: It's essential to estimate these costs, which include materials, advertising, taxes, utilities, and more. Always round up these estimates to create a financial buffer.

- Revenue Forecasting: To predict your monthly income, look at different sources like loans, credit lines, investments, and the money you expect to make from sales. Estimating sales requires thorough market research and an understanding of your target customers. To ensure accuracy, familiarize yourself with the market dynamics, competitor pricing, and customer preferences from your market research.

After calculating the costs outlined in your checklist, assessing whether your projected monthly revenue can adequately cover both fixed and variable expenses is crucial. This analysis will reveal your business's monthly operational costs, aiding in establishing realistic sales targets. Additionally, totaling your start-up expenses will determine the initial capital required to launch your business.

Navigating the complexities of budget creation and management calls for the right set of tools and resources, each designed to simplify the process and enhance accuracy. Budgeting software and templates are invaluable aids in this endeavor, automating calculations, organizing data, and providing visual representations of financial information.

Software solutions like Mint, YNAB (You Need A Budget), and PocketGuard offer platforms for meticulous budget tracking and analysis tailored to meet the needs of start-ups and small businesses. These tools facilitate the creation of detailed budgets and enable real-time financial performance monitoring against set benchmarks.

Templates, available through platforms such as Microsoft Excel and Google Sheets, provide a structured foundation for budget creation. These customizable resources allow entrepreneurs to input their specific financial data, adjusting categories and projections to fit the unique contours of their business.

In harnessing these tools and resources, entrepreneurs equip themselves with the means to craft realistic, comprehensive, and adaptable budgets. This adaptability ensures that the budget remains a living document, evolving in step with the business and serving as a constant guide in the journey toward financial stability and success.

Mixing personal and business finances can complicate your start-up's financial situation, leading to potential legal issues and making tax filing more difficult. To avoid these problems, separating your finances from the beginning is vital. This separation not only simplifies tax preparation by keeping business transactions clear but also protects you legally by distinguishing your personal assets from those of your business. Additionally, maintaining separate finances enhances your start-up's professionalism in the eyes of investors, partners, and customers. If you use personal funds to kickstart your business, ensure these are documented as formal investments in both your personal and business records.

The selection of a bank and the type of account opened is not a decision to be made lightly because it influences your day-to-day financial transactions and the strategic financial management of the start-up. Considerations extend beyond mere convenience or low fees. The chosen institution should offer services that align with the needs of the business, from online banking capabilities and merchant services to lines of credit and loan options. Furthermore, the type of account, whether a standard business checking account or a more specialized account tailored to start-ups, should reflect the volume of transactions, the need for interest accrual on balances, and the potential for future financial services.

Cash flow is crucial for a start-up, acting as its financial backbone. It's imperative to not only keep an eye on the inflow and outflow of cash but also skillfully manage these transactions' timing. A well-managed cash flow strategy includes efficient billing processes, ensuring client payments are received promptly, carefully scheduling bill payments to avoid late fees, and planning for significant expenses. Furthermore, establishing a cash reserve is essential. This reserve acts as a safety net, helping your business navigate through tough times without affecting its growth or day-to-day operations.

Navigating the complex financial landscape of a start-up can be daunting. Yet, seeking advice from financial experts is a prudent move, not a sign of weakness. Their guidance in budgeting, cash flow management, revenue forecasting, tax planning, and compliance is invaluable. By tapping into their expertise, you can preemptively address potential financial challenges, ensuring a robust and adaptable financial strategy for your start-up.

Financial planning is a crucial foundation for any start-up, integrating budgeting, forecasting, strategic banking choices, and professional advice. This solid groundwork enables a start-up to tackle the financial hurdles of entrepreneurship with confidence, making well-informed decisions every step of the way.

> **Action Step:** Create your start-up budget.

## Understanding Taxes: What You Need to Know

Understanding the complex world of taxes is crucial for any business owner. Taxes vary widely depending on the type of business and where it's located. They are essential payments for the privilege of running a business, requiring careful planning and strategy to reduce costs while following the law.

Navigating the complexities of business taxation requires a keen understanding of various tax types, each with its unique set of rules and implications.

**Income tax**, representing the share of profits paid to the government, is a consistent aspect of business operations. However, its rate and application can significantly differ by location. Businesses face a layered system of income taxes that includes federal, state, and occasionally local levels, each introducing specific rates and rules.

**Sales tax** adds a layer of complexity to business operations, being applied at the point of sale for goods and services. This tax becomes particularly challenging for businesses operating across different jurisdictions, as each state has specific sales tax rates and rules, thereby complicating compliance efforts.

**Payroll tax**, a charge on employee earnings, highlights the investment in your workforce. This includes the complexity of handling withholding requirements, contributions to

Social Security and Medicare, and other employment taxes. Navigating through these requirements emphasizes the need for thorough tracking and payment systems.

Meticulous record-keeping is crucial for tax compliance, strategic planning, and dispute resolution in the business world. Effective tax record management involves more than saving receipts; it demands a systematic method to accurately document transactions, expenses, and income. Digital tools and software significantly aid this process, simplifying expense tracking, transaction organization, and report generation to facilitate tax preparation and strategic financial planning.

Beneath the surface of tax responsibilities, there's a silver lining: the chance to lower your tax bill through deductions and credits. These tools help lessen the financial load. Deductions let you decrease your taxable income by accounting for various business expenses, from daily operational costs such as rent and utilities to growth-driven expenditures like marketing efforts and professional training. On the other hand, credits directly reduce the taxes you owe, rewarding your business for engaging in specific activities, including research and development projects or making eco-friendly investments.

Particularly for small businesses, mastering tax deductions and credits can shift their tax strategy from merely defensive to decidedly strategic. The tax code has many deduction opportunities, ranging from home office costs for individual entrepreneurs to asset depreciation for more complex corporations.

The intricate nature of tax laws, combined with the importance of compliance and the possibilities for financial optimization, highlight the crucial role of professional tax advice. Accountants and tax professionals go beyond just completing paperwork and meeting deadlines; they provide valuable strategic guidance. Their deep understanding of complex tax regulations enables them to identify potential savings, assist in planning for future financial obligations, and mitigate risks. Their expertise is especially critical during audits, where their ability to maintain detailed records and implement strategic tax planning can turn a challenging situation into a straightforward demonstration of compliance.

Beyond simple compliance, the world of taxes is about actively engaging with the financial framework essential to your business's success. This requires more than just following rules. It calls for a forward-thinking approach to planning, diligent record-keeping, and seeking expert advice. By doing so, managing taxes transforms from a daunting task into a strategic benefit for your business.

## Protecting Your Business: Insurances

Starting a business means facing risks and uncertainties. Being well-prepared and forward-looking is crucial, and securing insurance is a key part of this preparation. Insurance serves as a safeguard against unexpected events, providing protection for your business's financial health, assets, and employees. The variety of business insurance options available offers tailored coverage against diverse risks, ensuring your business can safely innovate and grow.

Navigating the spectrum of insurance options begins with understanding the fundamental coverages available and their relevance to your business operations.

**Liability insurance**, a cornerstone of business protection, guards against claims arising from injury or damage caused by the business's operations or products. Within this category, specialized forms such as professional liability insurance address the unique risks associated with specific professions, offering protection against claims of negligence or malpractice.

**Property insurance** envelops the business's physical assets in a protective embrace, shielding against loss or damage due to events like fire, theft, or natural disasters. This coverage extends beyond just buildings to include equipment, inventory, and even the loss of income resulting from an interruption in operations.

**Workers' compensation insurance** is for businesses that rely on human talent, and it provides an essential safety net, covering medical expenses and lost wages for employees injured on the job. This coverage is not merely a financial safeguard but a legal requirement in many jurisdictions.

Determining the appropriate insurance coverage for your business is a task that demands a detailed approach and balances the specific risks inherent in your industry with the scale and scope of your operations. A restaurant, with its bustling kitchen and constant flow of customers, faces a different set of risks compared to a software development firm, where intellectual property and data security might be of paramount concern. Conducting a thorough risk assessment, therefore, becomes the first step in tailoring your insurance coverage. This process involves an inventory of physical and intangible assets and a critical evaluation of operational vulnerabilities.

Once you've identified your insurance needs, it's time to seek the right provider. This step requires careful research and attention to detail. You'll need to compare what different insurers offer regarding coverage options, how much they charge (premium costs), and whether they're financially stable. However, it's not just about the numbers. Customer service and support quality are just as important, especially when it's time to make a claim. Getting recommendations from other business owners and reading online reviews can help you gauge an insurer's reliability and how responsive they are. These insights will help you find an insurance provider that meets your business's specific needs and shares your values.

Insurance needs to change alongside your business's growth and shifts in direction. Regularly updating your insurance policies ensures they match your evolving operations and cover emerging risks. This proactive approach aligns your coverage with your business's needs, effectively safeguarding your expanding assets and operations.

In the unpredictable business world, insurance is an investment in your business's future, acting as a safety net for unforeseen challenges. This enables you to focus on growth and improvement. The process involves selecting the right types of insurance, accurately determining your needs, choosing a reliable provider, and consistently updating your coverage to fit your evolving business. Each step forms a protective cycle that safeguards your business's financial health and ensures operational stability, no matter the circumstances.

As we move from the initial steps of planning, structuring, and protecting your business, our focus shifts toward making your vision a reality. The path forward will explore strategies and actions that transform your ideas into tangible outcomes. This next section is all about putting your plans into practice, turning the conceptual framework of your business plan into concrete products, services, and customer experiences. At this juncture, the foundational work in understanding business structures, managing finances, navigating taxes, and securing insurance come together, paving the way for fulfilling your entrepreneurial dream.

**Action Step:** Determine what aspect of your business needs protection and what insurance coverage you will need.

# Chapter Three

# Securing and Understanding Start-up Funding

At the beginning of your business journey, traditional funding methods may seem promising but often prove difficult to access. Securing the capital necessary to transform your idea into reality requires determination and innovative thinking. This chapter explores alternative funding options that, while less conventional, provide opportunities for those willing to venture beyond traditional routes. Here, choosing the unconventional becomes a deliberate strategy, presenting both challenges and possibilities.

## Creative Funding Options for Start-Ups

The alternative funding landscape is diverse, each with unique characteristics, advantages, and challenges.

**Crowdfunding** platforms like Kickstarter invite many individuals to play a part in realizing a business idea, offering a dual benefit: the validation of the concept by potential customers and the capital to make it a reality. However, the success of a crowdfunding campaign hinges on compelling storytelling and robust marketing efforts to capture the imagination and open the wallets of the crowd.

**Angel investors**, affluent individuals seeking to invest in promising start-ups, offer funding, invaluable mentorship, and access to networks. Securing an angel investor requires a solid business plan and a clear demonstration of the potential for significant returns on their investment. The challenge here lies in finding the right match, where the investor's expertise and interests align with the start-up's domain.

**Venture capital** firms, though more challenging to sway, provide substantial amounts of capital and strategic assistance to scale businesses with high growth potential. The price, however, is often a significant share of equity and a say in business decisions, making it crucial for start-ups to weigh the benefits against the loss of control and autonomy.

**Strategic partnerships**, forming partnerships with established companies, can open up avenues for funding that also come with added benefits, such as access to resources, expertise, and customer bases. Such partnerships often emerge from a synergy between the start-up's innovative solutions and the established company's strategic goals or gaps in offerings. The art lies in identifying potential partners whose objectives align with the start-up's vision and negotiating terms that respect the interests and autonomy of both parties.

**Customer pre-orders** are a testament to the power of a compelling product and a well-crafted value proposition. By offering customers the opportunity to purchase products before they are manufactured, start-ups can generate the capital needed for production while also validating market demand. This approach requires a transparent communication strategy and a clear plan for production and delivery to maintain trust and satisfaction among early supporters.

**Start-up competitions** and **incubators** offer more than just prize money or seed funding. They provide platforms for networking, mentorship, and exposure to potential investors. Winning or simply participating in such competitions can lend credibility and visibility to a start-up, opening doors to further funding and partnership opportunities. Incubators, on the other hand, offer a nurturing environment for start-ups to refine their business models and strategies with the support of experienced mentors. The challenge lies in the competitive application processes and, for incubators, the potential equity stake required in return for their support.

Here is a **decision tree** to assist in the decision-making process for selecting an appropriate funding source and exploring the best fit based on their current stage, funding needs, and strategic goals.

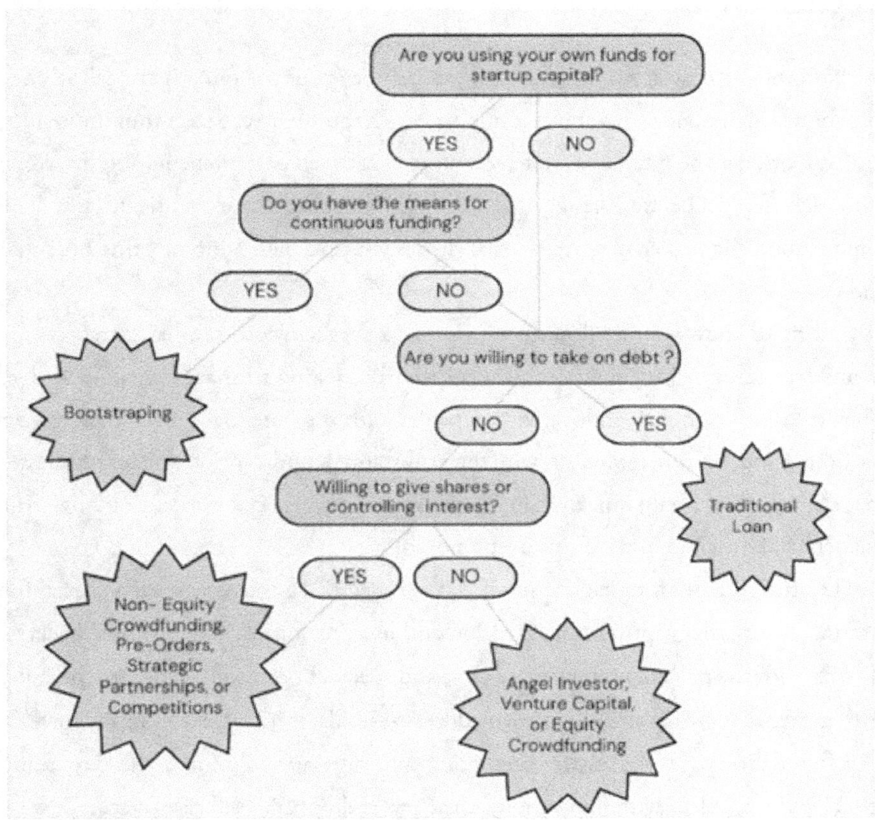


This section unravels the complex world of alternative funding, arming entrepreneurs with essential insights to navigate the intricacies of start-up financing. Each funding option brings unique advantages and challenges, demanding careful consideration and planning. The choice of funding profoundly impacts a start-up's trajectory, influencing its financial stability, growth, and autonomy. In the dynamic landscape of start-up funding, success hinges on creativity, perseverance, and strategic choices.

## Crafting a Compelling Pitch: Winning Over Venture Capital and Angel Investors

In the competitive world of start-ups, mastering the art of the pitch is crucial. It's not just about selling an idea; it's about connecting with those who can turn your dream into reality. Consider the pitch as a strategic interplay between entrepreneurs and investors, with each step deliberately designed to highlight possible gains and mitigate risks. The pitch embodies a powerful narrative that distills your business concept's true potential and value.

Getting to know your audience is the first step. Angel investors, often entrepreneurs themselves, are not just looking to invest; they're looking to share their knowledge. They're attracted to new, innovative companies with the potential for big returns. On the other hand, venture capitalists, with their substantial funds, are looking for businesses that are ready to scale up quickly. They invest with a strategic eye, focusing on how their financial stake might grow in value over time.

The structure of an impactful pitch is composed of key elements, each crucial for crafting a story that captures the attention and imagination of your potential backers. It starts with the problem statement, a clear and succinct portrayal of the current issue, setting the scene by highlighting the unaddressed needs or inefficiencies in the market. This foundation paves the way for presenting your start-up's solution as the hero, ready to tackle the problem with innovation, efficiency, and unparalleled ease of access. Next, we expand the narrative to include market potential, illustrating a market that is ready for change, where your start-up's solution doesn't just fit in but stands out, promising attractive returns for investors. The team behind the venture is introduced as its core strength, a fusion of diverse skills, experiences, and the drive necessary to turn the vision into reality. This collective expertise and passion reinforce the start-up's capability to achieve its ambitious goals.

Integrating storytelling into your pitch transforms it from a simple presentation to an immersive experience. It emotionally engages investors, making your start-up's journey a part of their understanding. This approach incorporates data and insights into a narrative of trials, triumphs, and aspirations. Investors are drawn to this narrative, recognizing the real people and passion behind the numbers. The strength of your story lies in its truthfulness, the honest depiction of your founders' adventures, the development of your solution, and the change you aim to make.

Preparation for the inevitable questions post-pitch demands familiarity with one's venture and a strategic anticipation of investor concerns. Questions often probe the viability of the business model, the scalability of the solution, the competitive landscape, and the exit strategy. Each inquiry tests the founders' grasp of their business and their ability to navigate potential hurdles. The readiness to tackle these questions with clarity, confidence, and data-backed precision speaks volumes, transforming potential doubts into affirmations of the start-up's solidity and the founders' intelligence.

The pitch deck, acting as the visual counterpart to your story, plays a critical role in bringing your business vision to life. It's not about having a multitude of slides but focusing on their quality, each one finely tuned to reflect the essential elements of your venture. A well-crafted pitch deck balances visual appeal and informative content, employing graphics and data to highlight key points while removing unnecessary details that could detract from your core message. Essential components such as the problem you're addressing, your solution, market analysis, business model, team capabilities, and financial projections are the pillars of your deck. Each slide should be designed to deliver these insights with precision and impact. The true skill in developing a pitch deck is in its capacity to captivate the audience, leading them through your entrepreneurial journey visually and cognitively and leaving them well-informed and genuinely moved by your proposition.

In sum, crafting a pitch that resonates with angel investors and venture capitalists is a meticulous blend of strategy, storytelling, and design. This process requires a profound insight into your audience's expectations, a compelling explanation of your business's unique benefits, and the flexibility to adeptly address investors' critical evaluations. The pitch is not just a presentation but a bridge, connecting the realms of innovation and investment and transforming the potential of ideas into the reality of funded ventures.

## Crowdfunding Success: A Strategy Guide

In the realm of start-up financing, crowdfunding is a versatile tool, morphing to fit the contours of diverse projects and ambitions. It operates through platforms that aggregate small contributions from a broad audience and funnels them into a single financial stream capable of turning concepts into market-ready products or services.

Within this framework, donation-based crowdfunding appeals to the philanthropic spirit, allowing contributors to support projects without expecting a financial return. Rewards-based crowdfunding, on the other hand, offers tangible incentives, from early product versions to exclusive experiences, aligning backer contributions with concrete benefits. Meanwhile, equity crowdfunding stands as a beacon for those seeking to support and invest, offering a slice of ownership in exchange for funding. Understanding the mechanics and appeal of each type provides the foundation for selecting the most aligned route for your start-up's funding journey.

Selecting a crowdfunding platform is a decision that parallels the importance of choosing a business location in the physical world. Platforms like Kickstarter and Indiegogo have risen to prominence, offering a broad reach and a track record of successful campaigns, particularly for rewards-based crowdfunding. For those leaning toward equity crowdfunding, platforms like SeedInvest and Crowdcube present a more focused audience of potential investors willing to exchange capital for equity. The decision hinges on thoroughly analyzing each platform's user base, fee structure, success rates, and compatibility with your start-up's industry and funding objectives. The goal is to find an area where your project's appeal meets the platform's strengths, maximizing visibility and engagement among potential backers.

In the world of crowdfunding platforms, creating a campaign that truly stands out demands authenticity, a clear vision, and a touch of creativity. At the core of this effort is developing a compelling story. This story should highlight the problem your start-up is solving and resonate emotionally with potential backers. Utilizing video as a medium can be particularly effective here, providing a vibrant platform to introduce your team, showcase your product, and share your vision. Equally important is the design of your reward tiers. This requires careful consideration to ensure they are both appealing and realistic. Designing rewards that increase in value, from simple "thank yous" to unique experiences, can attract a wider range of contributors. This approach also helps build a community of backers who feel valued and included in your start-up's journey.

Cultivating a community around your crowdfunding campaign transforms passive viewers into active supporters, engendering a sense of participation and investment in your start-up's success. Social media platforms are vital for this engagement, offering forums for regular updates, behind-the-scenes glimpses, and direct interaction with backers. The key is in consistent communication, incorporating the campaign into ongoing conversations, and leveraging the power of storytelling to maintain interest and momentum. Engagement extends beyond the digital realm, incorporating live events, webinars, or Q&A sessions to deepen connections with your audience, offering them a stake in the product and the journey of creation itself.

The conclusion of a crowdfunding campaign is not the end but a transition, shifting from pursuing funds to fulfilling promises. This phase underscores the importance of transparency and reliability, as the timely delivery of rewards and the continuous flow of updates cement the trust placed in you by backers. It's a period where meticulous planning meets execution, requiring a detailed roadmap for production, fulfillment, and communication. Regular updates, whether celebrating milestones or acknowledging delays, sustain the dialogue with your backers, preserving the community's spirit and support cultivated during the campaign. It's a testament to the principle that in crowdfunding, backers invest not just in a product but in the people and the narrative behind it.

The journey of crowdfunding success is vividly brought to life through real-world case studies, shining as examples for future entrepreneurs.

> Pebble is an innovative smartwatch that transitioned from relative anonymity in the crowdfunding scene to significant market success. Its campaign didn't just exceed its funding targets; it also established a solid foundation for the product's eventual commercial triumph.

> Flow Hive project leveraged rewards-based crowdfunding to revolutionize beekeeping, offering backers a stake in environmental sustainability and the tangible benefit of easier honey harvesting.

These examples underscore the potential of crowdfunding to serve as a launchpad for innovation, provided that campaigns are crafted with precision, engage audiences effectively, and fulfill their commitments with integrity.

## Bootstrapping Your Way to Success: Funding Your Business Yourself

Self-funding, also known as bootstrapping, is more than just a way to finance your business—it's a philosophy. It embodies the qualities of being resourceful, independent, and deeply committed to your business idea. This route requires a lot of discipline and personal sacrifice but brings significant benefits. One of the biggest advantages is maintaining complete control over your business decisions, free from the influence or demands of outside investors. Additionally, bootstrapping helps to keep debt at bay, protecting your emerging business from the heavy weight of financial obligations that could hinder its ability to grow and innovate.

Bootstrapping requires smartly managing every dollar. A cornerstone of this approach is cutting down expenses, but it's not just about slashing costs left and right. It's about adopting a lean mindset, scrutinizing every outlay to see if it's truly necessary, and seeking out more affordable, or even free, alternatives whenever possible. This careful evaluation often reveals opportunities to bypass traditional expenses by embracing innovative solutions, like opting for lower-cost or complimentary digital tools instead of pricier services.

Reinvesting profits represents another pillar of bootstrapping, a cycle where the fruits of the start-up's labors are plowed back into the business, fueling its growth in a self-sustaining loop. This strategy accelerates expansion and reinforces the start-up's financial health, gradually building a reservoir of resources that can support more ambitious projects or cushion against unforeseen financial shocks.

The reallocation of personal savings toward the start-up's funding pool is a testament to the entrepreneur's commitment and belief in their vision. While present with personal risk, this move underscores the confidence in the start-up's potential and often serves as a compelling narrative that strengthens the team's resolve and attracts future investments or partnerships based on the founder's demonstrated dedication.

Making use of free resources is a key strategy for bootstrappers, ranging from employing open-source software to leveraging social media for marketing at no cost and even initiating trade deals with suppliers or service providers. This approach saves money and cultivates a mindset of innovation and adaptability in the start-up, qualities crucial for thriving through the challenges of business expansion.

Maintaining a balance between growing your business and keeping it financially stable is important, especially when you're funding it yourself. You want your business to grow, but not faster than your finances can handle. To avoid stretching your resources too thin and putting your business at risk, it's wise to adopt a gradual growth strategy. This means planning your expansion in small, manageable steps that are supported by the funds you already have. This approach ensures your growth is steady and based on your business's real achievements, not just hopeful guesses. It's about ensuring every step forward is sustainable and adds value, keeping your business solid and ready for the future.

The history of business is filled with stories of companies that started with little and climbed their way to the top. These stories motivate and offer valuable lessons for those starting with their own funding. Take Dell, for instance. This tech behemoth started in a university dorm room with hardly any initial investment. Michael Dell, its founder, utilized a direct sales model and a build-to-order approach for computers, reinvesting the profits to foster growth. This strategy was key to elevating the company to a global leadership position.

Similarly, the story of Spanx, founded by Sara Blakely with her savings, underscores the power of a singular product and sheer determination. Blakely's hands-on approach, from patenting the product herself to personally pitching it to retailers, exemplifies the bootstrapping spirit. She leveraged personal resources, embraced direct involvement in every facet of the business, and meticulously reinvested earnings to drive expansion.

These success stories illuminate the path for aspiring entrepreneurs, offering proof of concept for the bootstrapping model and practical insights into its application. They reveal common threads of lean operation, creative resource utilization, phased growth, and unwavering commitment to the vision, each element a critical component of the bootstrapping success formula.

Bootstrapping is a comprehensive approach to organically growing your business. This method hinges on a steadfast belief in your idea, the readiness to invest personal funds, and the smart balancing of growth with fiscal responsibility. By managing expenses wisely, reinvesting earnings, using personal savings strategically, and leveraging free resources, bootstrapping paves the way to success. It grants full control over your enterprise, reduces debt, and fosters a culture of innovation and resilience. The triumph of businesses that have adopted this strategy showcases that bootstrapping is an all-encompassing journey that endows your business with independence, creativity, and a deep-seated dedication to your entrepreneurial vision.

## Small Business Loans: A Traditional Approach

In the world of start-up financing, small business loans are a classic and reliable option, providing essential support to new businesses. Despite the challenges and strict requirements often involved, they are a fundamental choice for entrepreneurs looking to build a strong base for their business. The variety of small business loans available is designed to suit the unique needs of different types of businesses, making them a versatile option for funding.

The variety of small business loans serves as a toolkit for entrepreneurs, each type catering to different needs and stages of business development.

**SBA loans**, supported by the Small Business Administration, offer advantageous terms and rates specifically to support start-ups and small businesses that might struggle to secure traditional funding.

**Traditional bank loans** demand thorough preparation and strong credibility due to their strict criteria and collateral requirements, yet they provide a direct pathway to significant capital.

**Microloans** represent a niche option, targeting smaller or newer businesses that may not yet qualify for larger sums, offering vital funds that can be crucial for early growth and sustainability.

The journey to securing a small business loan starts with checking if you're eligible. This process is like a test, showing whether you're ready for formal financing. Lenders look closely at credit scores to see if you've been responsible with money before. They want to know you can handle this commitment. Your business plan is also crucial; it's your chance to show lenders your vision and how you plan to make it a reality. They'll look at this document closely. And don't forget about collateral! It's your way of reassuring lenders that you're serious and ready to back up your business dreams with something tangible.

Taking out a small business loan is a significant decision, much like standing at a crossroads where each path leads to different outcomes. The main attraction of these loans is their provision of immediate capital, which can enable growth and expansion by offering the liquidity needed for both day-to-day operations and strategic initiatives. However, accepting a loan also means accepting debt, which can impact your business's cash flow and limit financial freedom. The loan terms, including interest rates and repayment schedules, become critical elements of your business's financial planning, influencing how you manage your obligations and plan for the future.

Successfully navigating the world of small business loans requires more than just determination; it calls for careful planning and strategic thinking. Improving your credit score is an essential first step in the application process, demonstrating your financial responsibility and reliability to lenders. Equally important is developing a comprehensive business plan. This document should strike a balance between your ambitions and the practical realities of your market, presenting a well-rounded view of your business's potential. Additionally, understanding what lenders are looking for can help you tailor your application to meet their expectations, significantly increasing your chances of securing a loan.

In wrapping up this chapter, it's clear that funding options vary widely. Small business loans stand out for their reliability and strict criteria, providing essential capital for growth. However, they demand a blend of ambition and prudence. Successfully managing a loan can propel a small business to new heights. The path ahead involves exploring funding avenues aligning with our goals and ethical considerations and being ready to embrace opportunities and challenges. With the insights gained, we're better positioned to tackle the business landscape's complexities, moving forward with confidence and a clear vision for success.

**Action Step:** Use the decision tree and information in this chapter to determine the capital resource you will use.

# Chapter Four

# Financial Mastery for New Entrepreneurs

Facing financial management is crucial for entrepreneurs, bridging the gap between dreams and reality. While handling finances may appear tedious, it's essential for building a successful business. This chapter simplifies the complex world of accounting and financial management, ensuring your business grows and thrives.

## Basic Accounting

**Accounting**, a critical aspect of business management, is built on essential principles that every entrepreneur should understand. Picture organizing a dinner party where everything from the choice of ingredients to their precise timing plays a role in its success. Similarly, accounting demands strategically handling and examining financial elements—assets, liabilities, equity, revenue, and expenses—to safeguard your business's financial well-being.

**Bookkeeping**, the day-to-day tracking of financial activities, is the backbone of effective accounting. This diligent process is comparable to placing bricks to form a pathway, where each transaction is carefully recorded to support wider financial analysis and decision-making.

**Accuracy** in transaction recording is a best practice and the foundation of financial integrity and accountability. This precision ensures that every dollar spent or earned is accounted for, representing the business's financial health. It's like a chef meticulously measuring ingredients to ensure the final dish is flawless. Entrepreneurs should adopt a regimented approach to recording transactions, categorizing each meticulously and reviewing entries regularly to prevent discrepancies that could muddle financial analysis and decision-making.

**Financial statements**, such as the balance sheet, income statement, and cash flow statement, serve as the window through which the financial health of a business is viewed. Understanding these documents reveals a wealth of insights; the balance sheet captures the business's financial position at a specific point in time. The income statement, or profit and loss statement (P&L), tracks revenue and expenses over a period, telling the story of the business's operational performance. The cash flow statement, meanwhile, reveals the movement of cash in and out of the business, highlighting liquidity and operational efficiency. Together, they form a picture that offers a comprehensive view of the business's financial health and trajectory.

In the current digital era, entrepreneurs can access an abundance of accounting software designed to streamline financial management, from automating transactions to producing in-depth financial reports. Choosing the right accounting software for your start-up is crucial and depends on a detailed evaluation of your unique needs, including factors like cost, features, scalability, and ease of use. Notable examples include user-friendly platforms such as QuickBooks and FreshBooks and more comprehensive systems like Sage and Xero, each offering distinct functionalities to serve businesses of different sizes and sectors. The market is flush with tools and resources to simplify accounting tasks for business owners. These range from software that handles bookkeeping automatically to templates that ease the preparation of financial statements, allowing entrepreneurs to focus more on strategic decisions. The American Institute of CPAs (AICPA) website is an invaluable resource, providing guides, templates, and best practices specifically for small businesses. In addition, platforms like Khan Academy offer free tutorials on accounting fundamentals, providing a robust base for those wishing to enhance their accounting knowledge.

In this realm where numbers reign, an entrepreneur armed with accounting knowledge and the right tools stands poised to navigate the financial intricacies of their venture with confidence. Mastery over this domain ensures compliance and accuracy and unlocks strategic insights that drive informed decision-making, fueling the business's growth and success.

## Managing Start-Up Expenses: Cutting Costs without Cutting Corners

Managing a start-up's finances requires careful attention from entrepreneurs, who must find the right balance between saving money and making necessary investments. This section acts as a guide for wisely managing resources, showing business owners how to cut unnecessary costs while still supporting the growth and strength of their business.

Identifying unnecessary expenses is crucial for financial optimization in your start-up. View this process like sifting for gold—keep what's valuable and discard the rest. To enhance efficiency, scrutinize each expense for its contribution to your business objectives. Embrace regular financial reviews to eliminate non-contributory spending. Implementing zero-based budgeting, where every expense is justified for each new period, fosters a culture of financial prudence, transforming cost-saving from a goal to a core practice.

Another key strategy is leveraging economies of scale through bulk purchasing and forging long-term partnerships. This approach involves planning ahead and negotiating better deals for larger quantities or more favorable terms, aiming for mutual benefits like extended payment terms or flexible delivery options. The goal is not just to lower costs but to maintain quality, ensuring a win-win for both start-ups and suppliers.

Deciding between outsourcing tasks and handling them in-house is beneficial for cost management. This choice should balance the cost savings and quality benefits of outsourcing non-core activities with the potential challenges it brings, such as service integration and variability in quality. It's not just about cost but also how these decisions align with your business goals, enhance your capabilities, and preserve your team's essential skills.

In the toolkit of a budget-aware entrepreneur, technology emerges as a key force for streamlining and efficiency. Cloud services eliminate the expense of heavy IT setups, while Software as a Service (SaaS) models replace costly software licenses with more manageable monthly fees. These technological solutions can significantly lower operational costs. Yet, adopting technology smartly is essential. It involves choosing tools that fit your business needs and testing them to ensure they contribute positively to your operations. This strategic use of technology cuts costs and enhances your company's agility and financial health.

Seeking financial efficiency often leads down well-worn paths to expected results. Entrepreneurs, however, are encouraged to embrace innovation, exploring beyond conventional methods to discover new avenues for cost savings. This exploration could lead to innovative staffing approaches, such as utilizing freelance workers or interns, which can mitigate the costs of full-time employees. Another strategy is the barter system, trading goods or services directly with other businesses to fulfill mutual needs without exchanging money. Additionally, adopting remote or hybrid work models can drastically cut the overhead costs of maintaining physical office spaces. Each strategy highlights a key principle: the continuous drive for inventive cost management tactics that challenge the status quo and open up new possibilities.

Entrepreneurs take on a pivotal role in navigating a start-up's financial landscape, steering the company's spending and investment strategies. This guidance ensures that each expenditure is a strategic investment in the company's future rather than an unnecessary cost. By prioritizing eliminating unneeded expenses, smart purchasing decisions, a balanced approach to outsourcing versus in-house tasks, smart use of technology, and innovative cost-saving tactics, entrepreneurs can propel their businesses toward financial stability and growth. This process is about strategic planning and execution, not diminishing goals, enabling a path to success marked by thoughtful investment and financial efficiency.


## Managing Cash Flow in the Early Days

Understanding and managing cash flow is crucial at the beginning of a start-up's journey. Think of cash flow as the business's heartbeat, pumping money in and out, keeping it alive and growing. It's all about balancing what you earn against what you spend. Managing this balance is key to making sure your business can keep running smoothly and growing. Without careful attention to cash flow, a business risks running into financial trouble, potentially leading to failure.

To understand cash flow, you need to recognize its ever-changing nature. When cash flow is positive, it's a sign that the business is performing well, allowing you to meet various obligations like paying your employees and suppliers. On the other hand, when cash flow turns negative, it's a warning sign of financial difficulties, indicating that the business's expenses surpass its income. This realization highlights the critical need for careful cash flow management to ensure not just the survival of your business but its ability to flourish and seize new opportunities for growth.

Forecasting cash flow becomes an exercise in foresight, a projection of financial flow based on realistic assumptions of revenue generation and expenditure patterns. This process involves using past financial performance as a guide and setting a strategy that considers previous earnings and spending while preparing for possible changes in the business world. Entrepreneurs undertake this forward-looking task by predicting when and how much money will come in from sales or investments and comparing it to when and how much money will go out for things like operating expenses, paying back loans, and buying equipment or other assets. This forecasting highlights potential financial gaps or excesses, allowing for early actions to balance the business's finances.

Several tactics stand out for entrepreneurs who are pursuing a positive cash flow. Managing invoices effectively is crucial—by issuing them promptly and optimizing payment processes, you can shorten the time between making a sale and getting paid, thus keeping your financial cycle tight. Also, being strategic about when you spend money, such as delaying non-essential expenses until you have excess cash, helps maintain a safety net for unexpected costs. Controlling your inventory is equally important; keeping stock at optimal levels prevents your capital from being tied up in unsold items while still being able to promptly satisfy customer demand. Together, these strategies form a solid foundation of financial discipline and operational savvy, guiding your start-up through the initial hurdles of financial management.

In managing cash flow, dealing with late payments is a significant hurdle. These delays can disrupt your financial planning and may lead to a cash crunch. To tackle this problem, a balanced approach is necessary. This involves clear yet respectful communication with clients about payment expectations and exploring options for dealing with late payments, including negotiation. Offering incentives for early payments or imposing penalties for late payments can also be effective. Including these terms in contracts from the start can reduce confusion and encourage timely payments.

Unexpected expenses are like sudden storms that test how well you manage your cash flow. To handle these surprises, setting up an emergency fund is key. This fund acts as a safety net for unexpected situations, allowing your business to continue its operations and growth efforts without interruption. Creating this fund means consistently saving a bit of your positive cash flow and gradually building a financial cushion that protects your business from the unpredictable nature of finances.

Maneuvering through the early days of your start-up requires vigilant cash flow management to dodge financial pitfalls and ensure your business stays vibrant and solvent. Mastery of financial basics and a proactive planning and problem-solving mindset are key. By forecasting cash flows accurately, enforcing strict invoicing and spending policies, managing inventory efficiently, and creating an emergency fund, you can steer your business confidently through both stable and rough financial periods. This strategic cash flow management approach is critical for sustaining liquidity and driving steady business growth amidst financial challenges.

## Creating a Solid Financial Plan: Projections and Adjustments

Setting profitability goals is like navigating through unknown territories where your tools' accuracy and your vision's sharpness are critical. It's a complex task that demands a solid grasp of your business's inner workings and the competitive landscape you're part of. The process begins with a detailed review of your business's past financial performance, a competitor comparison, and an understanding of the industry norm. This review is not just about identifying what you're doing right or the opportunities you have; it's also about spotting weaknesses or inefficiencies that could block your path to profitability.

From here, the entrepreneur must distill this wealth of information into specific, quantifiable objectives. This isn't merely about setting a target for net income but about understanding the underlying drivers of profitability in your business. It may involve increasing revenue streams, improving operational efficiency, or reducing the cost of goods sold. Each objective must be grounded in realistic expectations and filled with the ambition necessary to drive progress. They must also be flexible and able to adapt as the business evolves and as new information comes to light.

Conducting a break-even analysis is a critical early step, serving as the foundation for a sustainable business model. It's the process of determining the point at which revenues equal costs, where the business neither makes a profit nor incurs a loss. This analysis requires a meticulous breakdown of fixed and variable costs, a task that demands understanding the nuances of your business's cost structure.

The understating of the break-even point offers invaluable insights, providing a clear target for sales and a benchmark for evaluating the feasibility of pricing models. It also plays a crucial role in financial forecasting, serving as a baseline for project future profitability and growth. Entrepreneurs must approach this analysis critically, questioning every assumption and refining their understanding of cost behavior in relation to sales volume.

Developing accurate financial projections is a challenging yet fulfilling process that blends detailed analysis with imaginative prediction. This task goes beyond just extending past trends into the future; it involves a deep dive into how market forces, competition, and strategic actions might influence your business. Your revenue forecasts should be based on real market conditions, considering an in-depth evaluation of your target market's size, how deeply you can penetrate it, and the average sales cycle length. Similarly, your expense forecasts need to account for the ongoing fixed costs of running your business and the variable costs of production and sales.

This process also includes forecasting cash flow, a critical element highlighting the timing and magnitude of cash inflows and outflows. Entrepreneurs should employ a conservative approach, preparing for the worst-case scenario while striving for the best. This approach ensures that the business is well-prepared to navigate the uncertainties of the market, equipped with a financial plan that is both robust and responsive.

A start-up's financial plan isn't set in stone; it's a living, breathing guide that should adapt as the business and the market evolve. It's crucial to periodically revisit this plan to make necessary updates informed by real-world performance and fresh insights. This could mean adjusting sales goals after receiving customer feedback, tweaking cost estimates after renegotiating with suppliers, or altering investment strategies due to shifts in cash flow.

Entrepreneurs must embrace this process of continuous refinement, viewing each adjustment not as a deviation from the plan but as a necessary step toward greater accuracy and relevance. It's a practice that demands open-mindedness, flexibility, and a commitment to data-driven decision-making.

Scenario planning is a powerful tool in the entrepreneur's arsenal, allowing for the exploration of different future states and their potential impact on the business. This process involves creating detailed models for a range of scenarios, from the most optimistic to the most pessimistic. Each scenario should be grounded in plausible assumptions about market conditions, customer behavior, and broader economic trends.

This approach enables entrepreneurs to anticipate challenges, identify opportunities, and develop contingency plans that ensure the business remains resilient in the face of uncertainty. It encourages strategic thinking, pushing beyond the confines of the current business model to explore new growth avenues and risk mitigation strategies.

The health of a start-up is mirrored in the metrics it tracks, where each number tells a story of progress, challenge, or opportunity. Entrepreneurs must identify the key financial metrics that are most indicative of their business's performance and health. These might include gross margin, net profit margin, customer acquisition cost, and cash burn rate.

Regular monitoring of these metrics provides a real-time snapshot of the business's financial status, enabling timely interventions when necessary. It's a practice that requires diligence and a deep understanding of the interplay between different financial indicators and their implications for overall business health. By keeping a close eye on these metrics, entrepreneurs can navigate their ventures with greater confidence and precision, steering toward profitability and sustainable growth.

## Financial Pitfalls to Avoid as a New Entrepreneur

Understanding the financial aspects of starting a business is crucial, but it's equally important to recognize the potential pitfalls that can threaten your business's success. These challenges might not always be obvious, often disguised as traditional advice or hidden by one's own ambitions. By being aware and proactive, entrepreneurs can navigate these obstacles effectively, ensuring a stable path toward lasting success.

Business start-up journeys are often marked by financial missteps, serving as crucial lessons for the ambitious entrepreneur. A common mistake is the underestimation of start-up costs. This optimistic view can lead to a harsh reality check when expenses exceed initial budgets, forcing the business into a desperate search for extra funding. Poor cash flow management is another significant hurdle, with the inability to balance income and expenses threatening the business's operational viability and increasing the risk of failure. Additionally, the temptation for rapid expansion can divert attention and stretch resources too thin, weakening the business's fundamental structure.

While borrowing money can help your business grow, relying too much on loans can trap you in a cycle of obligations that limit your ability to be creative and adapt. It's important to balance the money you've borrowed and the money invested in your business. This balance helps ensure that your business can grow without being too vulnerable to market changes or interest rate shifts.

Maintaining strict financial discipline is often overlooked in the excitement of growing a business. However, it's crucial for protecting against common financial challenges. Keeping personal and business finances separate is a basic rule, yet it's often ignored, leading to potential legal and tax issues. Similarly, avoiding unnecessary expenses and closely examining every cost to ensure it aligns with your business goals can prevent wasteful spending. This careful management of finances strengthens your business, making it more resilient against financial missteps.

In starting a business, encountering failure doesn't mean the end; rather, it serves as a powerful tool for growth and improvement. When faced with a reflective mindset and a readiness to learn, financial challenges transform into valuable lessons that sharpen an entrepreneur's skills. This learning process from financial difficulties requires a strong willingness to persevere and an openness to change tactics, adjust goals, and seek out new, creative solutions. Through this continuous cycle of trying, assessing, and refining, businesses gradually develop, strengthened by the knowledge gained from previous errors and encouraged by the insights from each setback.

In the complex entrepreneurship journey, avoiding the common financial pitfalls that often ensnare new business owners is essential. Wisdom and foresight are critical in steering clear of the dangers associated with underestimating costs, over-relying on debt, and mismanaging funds. Learning from failures and missteps is not a sign of defeat but a stepping stone to building a resilient and successful business. By being vigilant and adaptable, entrepreneurs can ensure their businesses survive and flourish in the competitive business world. Though filled with challenges, this path leads to a future of sustainability and achievement for those who are prepared to learn and evolve.

**Action Step:** Adjust your initial start-up budget and financial plan as needed.

# Chapter Five

# Branding and Start-Up Marketing

In today's fiercely competitive market, the power of a strong brand cannot be understated. It acts as a guiding light, leading customers through the noise and elevating branding from a simple task to an essential investment in your start-up's core. Take the simple example of a cup of coffee; its real value doesn't just lie in the quality of beans or the method of brewing but in the narrative the brand weaves around it, whether that's a tale of luxury, a commitment to sustainability, or a sense of community belonging. The magic lies in a brand's ability to create a deeper connection with its audience, turning an ordinary coffee into an indispensable part of someone's morning routine.

Branding is essentially the transformative process that turns basic business ideas into brands with distinct personalities, meaningful connections, and dedicated followers. It involves clearly identifying and showcasing what your start-up fundamentally represents, ensuring that everything from your logo's colors to your customer service tone reflects your brand's core identity and principles. This chapter explores the key elements of building a brand that captures attention and embodies values that resonate deeply with your intended audience, attracting them toward your business.

# Defining Your Brand Identity

Creating a brand identity involves more than selecting a logo or a color scheme; it's about crafting a visual and emotional palette that communicates the essence of your business. This process begins with understanding your brand's core values and personality: Are you innovative and edgy or classic and reliable? From there, every element, from your logo design to your font choices, should reflect these traits. A useful exercise involves imagining your brand as a person and considering how they would speak, dress, and interact with your target audience. This persona guides all branding decisions, ensuring consistency and authenticity. Every brand has a story, a narrative that connects the business and its audience. This story shouldn't be a fabrication but a genuine account of why your business exists, the challenges it aims to solve, and the impact it strives to have. Much like how a well-told anecdote can make a speaker instantly more relatable and memorable at a dinner party, a compelling brand story can transform your business from a faceless entity into a cherished part of your customers' lives. Sharing this narrative across all platforms, from your website to your packaging, invites customers into your journey, building empathy and loyalty.

> **Action Step**: Complete the following step-by-step guide to uncover and articulate your brand's unique story and explore your origins, mission, and vision for the future. This will help start the thought process about what your brand stands for and how it should be perceived by others.

*****

### Step 1: Uncover Your Origins

How Did Your Brand Begin?

Who Are the Founders, and What Are Their Stories?

What Were the Initial Challenges?

### Step 2: Define Your Mission

What Is Your Brand's Purpose?

Who Are You Here to Serve?

How Do You Serve Them Differently?

**Step 3: Share Your Values**

What Are Your Core Values?

How Do Your Values Reflect in Your Daily Operations?

**Step 4: Envision Your Future**

What Is Your Vision for the Future?

How Are You Innovating?

How Will You Continue to Serve Your Community or Industry?

**Step 5: Craft Your Story**

Compile Your Responses

Tell Your Story

Share and Evolve Your Story

***

Now that you have defined your brand identity, it is important to note that consistency is the foundation for every interaction a customer has with your brand, from their initial website visit to the moment they open your product. It guarantees a seamless and unified experience across all encounters with your brand. This uniformity goes beyond just visual elements, touching on the tone of your messages, the ideals you uphold, and how you handle customer queries. Imagine it like visiting a beloved restaurant where, no matter what you order or when you visit, the quality and service level you anticipate remains constant. This level of consistency fosters trust and dependability, which are vital in establishing a strong brand presence.

A brand is not set in stone but a living entity evolving with its market, audience, and the world. Gathering and actively listening to customer feedback is crucial for this adaptive process. It's not merely about monitoring social media comments or customer reviews but engaging in meaningful dialogue with your audience. Ask for their input, understand their changing needs, and show that you value their opinions. This feedback loop not only aids in refining your brand but also deepens customer engagement, making your audience feel like active participants in your brand's journey. Moreover, staying attuned to broader market and cultural trends ensures your brand remains relevant and resonates with contemporary values and expectations.

## Websites and Social Media: Your Online Presence

In today's digital age, establishing a strong online presence is crucial for start-ups. It's about sharing information and telling your brand's story, engaging with customers, and building a community. This online presence, including websites and various social media platforms, should reflect your business's core values, mission, and what makes it unique. It's an essential part of connecting with your audience and promoting your brand effectively.

The rise of social media platforms has leveled the playing field regarding brand visibility, allowing start-ups to reach a broad audience without significant financial output. Each platform's distinct culture and user base offers unique opportunities for start-ups to make their mark and cultivate their communities. The secret to success here lies in creating content that engages and connects with your audience, sparking meaningful conversations, and building relationships on a budget. Using hashtags effectively, joining in on trending conversations, and taking advantage of platform-specific features like Instagram Stories or X (formerly Twitter) Polls can greatly extend your reach, all while bypassing the substantial costs associated with traditional advertising methods.

Navigating the social media landscape effectively requires aligning your efforts with your brand's identity and audience preferences. Choosing the right platforms is necessary; it's about where your ideal customers are most active. Once you've identified the best platforms, the next step is to create content that echoes your brand's voice and values. This could involve sharing insightful articles on LinkedIn, offering behind-the-scenes peeks on Instagram, or initiating vibrant discussions on Facebook. The goal is to do more than just broadcast your message; your content should foster engagement and cultivate a sense of community. Utilizing scheduling tools and analyzing platform-provided metrics allows for strategic posting and real-time strategy adjustments based on audience interaction, making your social media efforts both impactful and efficient.

The cornerstone of a start-up's online presence is its website, a digital storefront inviting visitors into your brand's world. Creating a website that mirrors the essence of your brand while ensuring user-friendliness requires meticulous planning and execution. Start with a blueprint that outlines the user journey and ensures that navigation is intuitive, information is accessible, and the call to action is clear. The design must be a visual echo of your brand identity, with a consistent use of colors, fonts, and imagery that reinforces brand recognition. Equally important is the responsiveness of the design, ensuring that the website offers a seamless experience across devices, from desktops to smartphones. Embedding social media feeds and incorporating a search engine optimization (SEO) strategy from the outset enhances visibility and engagement, transforming your website from a static brochure to a vibrant hub of interaction.

The gauging of your online presence's efficacy unfurls through the lens of analytics, a treasure trove of data that offers insights into audience behavior, engagement patterns, and campaign performance. Platforms come equipped with their own analytic tools, from Instagram Insights to Google Analytics for websites, each providing metrics that measure the success of your online strategy. KPIs such as website traffic, bounce rate, social media engagement rates, and conversion metrics paint a picture of successes and areas for improvement. This continuous process of measurement and refinement is not an exercise in number crunching but a strategic tool to align your online presence with your brand goals, ensuring that every post and webpage furthers your brand narrative and deepens customer engagement.

Creating a strong online presence for your start-up involves more than just setting up a website and social media accounts. It's about combining these platforms effectively to showcase your brand, connect with your audience, and understand their behaviors through analytics. This approach is about creating a unified strategy where your online activities support and enhance each other, helping your brand make a real difference to your target audience.

## Content Marketing: Educating Your Way to Sales

Content marketing is a key strategy in today's digital world, where countless voices fight for attention. Instead of just pushing ads, it focuses on consistently creating and sharing useful, relevant information. The goal is to draw in and keep a specific group of people interested, leading them toward actions that are profitable for your business. At its core, content marketing is about educating rather than persuading; it's a move from simply selling products to sharing knowledge, from dictating to teaching.

Creating a content marketing strategy begins with a deep dive into the psyche of your target demographic, an exploration aimed at uncovering not only their needs and wants but also their fears, challenges, and aspirations. Understanding your target audience deeply and ensuring your messaging aligns with your brand's core values and principles is crucial. This approach develops a strategy that combines insights, creativity, and strategic thinking.

Every piece of content, from blog posts and videos to infographics, acts as a messenger, delivering your brand's narrative across the digital realm to your target audience. This journey isn't random. Each content piece is a strategic step in a broader plan, aiming to move your audience from initial awareness to becoming brand advocates. To achieve this, it's crucial to deeply understand what your audience likes to see and how they engage with content. Adopting a flexible approach to creating content, one that allows for adjustments based on audience reactions and feedback is essential for success.

The variety of content types available for marketing is vast and varied, each serving a unique purpose in engaging, informing, and inspiring audiences. Blogs are foundational to content marketing, providing depth and flexibility while enhancing SEO. They help establish a brand's credibility and expertise. Videos, on the other hand, are powerful in their ability to capture attention and convey messages in an entertaining manner, spreading a brand's message widely. Infographics simplify complex information, using visual elements to present data, processes, or comparisons clearly and memorably, much like how visuals can make a concept more accessible.

This diversity demands a strategic approach to content creation, one that aligns the strengths and characteristics of each content type with the goals of your brand and your audience's preferences. It's a balancing act that requires a keen understanding of the nuances of each format and the ability to adapt your strategy based on performance and feedback.

Introducing SEO into your content marketing strategy is like igniting a fire under your efforts, turning hard work into significant results. Essentially, SEO is both a science and an art focused on boosting your content's visibility and findability online. This is especially crucial, considering most online journeys start with a search engine.

This process begins with keyword research—conducting a deep dive into the language and terms your target audience employs while searching for online information. This research informs not just the topics you choose but the language you use, incorporating keywords into your content in a way that feels natural and enhances readability. On-page optimization strategies, including meta descriptions and alt tags, serve as navigational aids for both search engines and users. They improve the overall user experience and signal to search engines the relevance and importance of your content.

Creating compelling content is only one half of the equation—distribution is the other. This phase is where strategy meets execution, when carefully crafted content is launched into the digital world, reaching the screens and capturing the attention of your target audience. This requires a multi-channel approach, leveraging not just your own platforms, such as your website and social media, but also earned and paid channels.

Email newsletters, for instance, serve as a direct line to your audience, delivering content straight to their inboxes, while social media platforms offer a stage for your content to be shared, discussed, and engaged with. Guest posting on reputable sites in your industry extends your reach and enhances your brand's authority and backlink profile. The choice of channels and tactics must be guided by a clear understanding of your audience's habits and preferences, ensuring that your content finds them where they are most receptive.

Measuring success in content marketing is clear-cut and dependent on metrics like website traffic, engagement rates, conversion rates, and lead generation. These metrics give us a clear view of how well our content is performing, highlighting what grabs our audience's attention and what doesn't. This isn't just an evaluation after the fact but an essential part of your strategy. It's a continuous feedback loop that helps you improve your content marketing, ensuring it stays goal-oriented, meets your audience's needs, and adapts to changes in the digital world.

## Guerrilla Marketing: Creative, Low-Cost Tactics

In today's marketing landscape, where innovation and creativity are key, guerrilla marketing stands out as a unique approach. It's not about having a big budget but about using imagination to make a lasting impression. Guerrilla marketing uses unexpected and unconventional methods to grab people's attention and make your brand memorable. It turns everyday settings and online spaces into opportunities for creative brand promotion.

Guerrilla marketing thrives on turning the mundane into the remarkable, seeking out everyday scenarios to serve as the backdrop for engaging brand narratives. This strategy aims to do more than just reach audiences; it aims to create a meaningful impact, fostering interactions that encourage discussion, sharing, and, ultimately, a deeper connection with the brand. It demands a deep grasp of societal trends and consumer habits, leveraging this knowledge to design experiences that are not just observed but experienced.

Successful campaigns stand as testaments to the power of guerrilla marketing, each a masterclass in creativity and impact. Here are some examples:

A local cafe that, instead of traditional advertising, leaves branded, reusable coffee cups in major city areas for passersby to find and keep.

A tech start-up that projects interactive games onto the sides of buildings, allowing players to control the action via their smartphones.

These examples underscore the guerrilla approach's core: creating engaging, unexpected encounters that incorporate the brand into the narrative of people's lives.

Planning a guerrilla marketing campaign is like navigating through unknown territories. It starts with establishing clear goals, which serve as a guide for all creative initiatives. Whether it's to boost brand recognition, introduce a new product, or simply generate excitement, every part of the campaign should align with these goals. Knowing your target audience is just as important as involving a deep dive into demographic and psychographic information to gather insights into their behaviors, preferences, and how they consume media. This understanding informs the campaign's creative approach, ensuring the message reaches the intended audience and resonates with them.

Yet, with innovation comes risk. The unconventional nature of guerrilla marketing, which makes it so compelling, also introduces challenges and considerations. The line between creativity and controversy can be thin, and crossing it can have adverse effects on brand perception. Campaigns must be designed with sensitivity to cultural and social norms, ensuring that they surprise and delight rather than shock or offend. Legal considerations also play a crucial role, so public spaces and intellectual properties should be handled with care to avoid infringements that can turn a creative triumph into a costly debacle.

Ethical considerations are paramount, ensuring that campaigns are rooted in honesty and transparency. Misleading tactics or those that invade privacy can erode trust and tarnish the brand's reputation. Thus, guerrilla marketing demands creativity and a considered approach that weighs the potential impact on the brand and its audience.

In this marketing realm, where the unexpected is the most potent tool, brands can reimagine their relationship with consumers. With its low costs and high impact, Guerrilla marketing offers a path for start-ups and established brands alike to cut through the noise of traditional advertising, making a lasting impression that transcends the moment of engagement. It is a testament to the power of creativity and a reminder that in the marketing world, the most significant resource is imagination and the courage to use it.

## Networking: Building Relationships that Matter

Networking is much more than just swapping business cards or connecting on LinkedIn. It's about building a network of relationships fundamental to any business's success. These connections can provide knowledge, opportunities, and shared growth. For entrepreneurs, this network includes clients, partners, mentors, supporters, and collaborators, all essential to the business's journey.

A strong business network offers numerous benefits, including mentorship that can guide you through uncertain times, partnership opportunities that grow from working together, and customer referrals that come from trust and satisfaction. This network helps spread your brand's message far and wide, integrating your business into the larger market scene.

Effective networking is all about being active, engaging with others, and helping each other out. As an entrepreneur, diving into networking starts with attending industry events like seminars and trade shows. These are opportunities to meet future partners, share ideas, and build valuable connections. Joining professional associations is also key. These groups provide access to a community of people in your field where you can learn from others, share your own experiences, and grow your network.

In today's digital era, online platforms have become invaluable by connecting entrepreneurs from different locations and time zones. Engaging actively is essential to make the most of these platforms. This means participating in discussions, sharing knowledge, and providing value without expecting anything in return. By doing so consistently and with genuine intent, you can build relationships that go beyond the digital space, setting the stage for real-world collaborations.

Networking fundamentally revolves around creating sincere connections and fostering relationships grounded in authenticity and mutual appreciation. This authenticity is the foundation of trust, a priceless and unique asset cultivated through regular, honest interactions. The emphasis is placed on contributing value, whether through sharing knowledge, offering resources, or providing support, without immediately expecting something in return. Over time, these carefully built relationships form a strong network, demonstrating the strength of true connection.

Growing your business through networking is all about balance and mutual benefit. It's not just about seeking help or advice from your contacts but also about being helpful and providing value to them. This two-way street of support and collaboration helps everyone involved. You create a vibrant network by working together on projects, sharing opportunities, and offering guidance. This approach ensures that as one grows, so do the others, embodying the idea that a rising tide lifts all boats.

Strategic partnerships are like the secret sauce of networking. They happen when two businesses come together because they have similar goals and can help each other succeed. To find the right partners, you must look for companies offering more than just short-term benefits. You're looking for ones that can grow and succeed with you over time. These partnerships can be about working together on marketing, creating products together, or even combining your brands for special projects. Making these partnerships work requires more than just agreeing on terms; both sides must be committed to the same goal and working together to make a bigger impact.

Having a strong network is crucial in the business world, where the future can seem uncertain and the way forward unclear. It acts like a compass and a guiding light, helping entrepreneurs navigate through difficulties and find new opportunities. This underscores the importance of building and maintaining relationships, which are key to creating lasting success in any business venture.

## Unlock the Power of Generosity: Make a Difference with Your Review

"Kindness is the key to happiness. The more we share, the more we grow."
- Unknown

People who give without expectation live longer, happier lives, and make more money. So if we've got a shot at that during our time together, I'm gonna try. To make that happen, I have a question for you... Would you help someone you've never met, even if you never got credit for it?

Who is this person you ask? They are like you. Or, at least, like you used to be. Less experienced, wanting to make a difference, and needing help, but not sure where to look.

Our mission is to make starting a business accessible to everyone. Everything we do stems from that mission. And, the only way for us to accomplish that mission is by reaching...well...everyone. This is where you come in. Most people do, in fact, judge a book by its cover (and its reviews). So here's my ask on behalf of a struggling entrepreneur you've never met:

Please help that aspiring business owner by leaving this book a review.

Your gift costs no money and less than 60 seconds to make real, but can change a fellow reader's life forever.

**Simply scan the QR code below to leave your review:**

Thank you from the bottom of my heart. Now, back to our regularly scheduled programming.

# Chapter Six

# Sales and Customer Excellence

In the fast-paced and competitive sales world, success goes beyond simple transactions to become a strategic endeavor. Picture yourself as an expert navigator of the market, skilled at capturing key opportunities for engagement, identifying the most promising prospects, and discovering valuable insights. Developing an effective sales strategy requires a thorough grasp of market complexities, a keen eye for potential openings, and the agility to adjust to changing environments. This chapter delves into the crucial role of a sales strategy in fostering business growth, emphasizing the importance of building connections with your audience that turn potential buyers into loyal customers.

## Creating an Effective Sales Strategy

Defining your unique value proposition (UVP) is one of the first steps in creating your sales strategy, which was defined during your Business Canvas creation. Your UVP guides potential customers through a competitive landscape, highlighting your product or service's standout features. It delivers a concise, compelling message that clearly articulates why your offering is precisely what your customers need. You determined this in a previous chapter.

Emphasizing your product or service's key benefits is like giving a first-time visitor a detailed city map. It involves highlighting well-known spots and uncovering the lesser-known gems that provide a deeper, more genuine experience. This task requires thoroughly examining what your offering brings to the table and converting those features into real advantages that align with your target audience's needs and challenges. The goal is to demonstrate not just the functionality of your product but its impact in making your customers' lives better, more convenient, or more enjoyable.

In setting sales goals, precision and realism are the twin pillars upon which effective strategies are built. It's not about aiming for the stars with no plan on how to get there but setting milestones that are ambitious yet achievable and grounded in data and insights about your market, competition, and capabilities. These goals should guide all sales activities, ensuring that every effort is aligned with the overarching growth and sustainability objectives.

Choosing the right sales channels can feel like finding your way through a complex maze, demanding sharp insights to identify paths that lead directly to your target audience. Each option, from online marketplaces and physical storefronts to resellers and direct sales, has unique advantages and challenges. Your decision should be informed by where your customers prefer to shop, the nature of your product or service, and the resources at your disposal. Your choice of sales channels should be flexible and evolving with market trends, consumer behavior, and the competitive landscape.

This comprehensive chart evaluates various sales channels based on factors such as reach, cost, control, and customer preference, which will help you determine the most effective avenues for your product or service.

| Channel Suitability Matrix | | | | |
|---|---|---|---|---|
| Sales Channel | Reach (High/Medium/Low) | Cost (High/Medium/Low) | Control (High/Medium/Low) | Customer Preference (High/Medium/Low) |
| Direct Sales | Medium | High | High | Medium |
| Retail | High | Medium | Medium | High |
| E-commerce | High | Low | High | High |
| Wholesale | High | Low | Low | Low |
| Distributors | High | Medium | Low | Medium |
| Partnerships | Medium | Variable | Medium | High |
| Affiliate Marketing | Medium | Low | Medium | Medium |
| Social Media | High | Low to Medium | Medium | High |
| Pop-up Shops | Low | Medium to High | High | Medium |
| Trade Shows | Medium | High | High | Medium |

In the realm of sales, data reigns supreme, offering insights that uncover the path to optimization and growth. Tracking and analyzing sales performance go beyond number crunching; it's about deciphering the story behind the figures. Which products are flying off the shelves, and which are stagnating? What patterns emerge during different seasons or across different regions? This analysis highlights areas for improvement and uncovers opportunities for innovation and expansion. The meticulous tracking of sales data ensures that your strategies always nurture the bottom line.

The continuous evaluation of your UVP stands as a testament to the complex nature of the market. Feedback from customers, shifts in market trends, and the emergence of new competitors all serve as valuable inputs that can refine and strengthen your value proposition. This process is not about reinventing the wheel but polishing it, ensuring it remains the most compelling choice in a crowded marketplace. It underscores the importance of agility in business, the ability to evolve and adapt, ensuring that your sales strategy remains relevant and effective.

> **Action Step**: Decide on a mix of channels that offers the best balance for your business goals, taking into account the resources you have available.

## Sales Funnel Basics: From Awareness to Purchase

The sales funnel, a strategic model, encapsulates a potential customer's journey from their initial interaction with your brand to the pivotal moment of purchase. This funnel, while seemingly straightforward, is layered with complexity, each stage demanding a unique approach to gently guide the lead closer to becoming a valued customer.

At its core, the sales funnel consists of several key stages: awareness, interest, decision, and action. In the awareness phase, potential customers first encounter your brand. Envision the initial encounter with your brand as a moment of ignition, where the customer's curiosity is sparked, and a path of engagement begins. As potential customers advance to the interest stage, this spark evolves into a keen interest and a growing desire to delve deeper into what you have to offer. As they progress into the decision phase, their interest intensifies, driven by a strong need or want, as they contemplate a purchase. Finally, reaching the action stage, this journey reaches its zenith as interest solidifies into a definitive choice, finalizing the decision to make a purchase.

Attracting potential customers to the top of the sales funnel is similar to spreading a wide net, crafted with messages that resonate and placed where your target audience is most active. In this phase, leveraging content marketing and social media advertising is crucial. By creating engaging blog posts, informative videos, and eye-catching social media campaigns, you can capture the interest of a diverse group of potential customers. However, the real skill is developing content that does more than just capture attention.

It should connect on a personal level, sparking not only interest but also a genuine connection. This initial engagement leads potential customers into the funnel and starts them on their path to making a purchase.

Once within the funnel, the focus shifts to nurturing these leads, steadily providing a mix of information, engagement, and persuasion. At this stage, targeted content plays a pivotal role, offering tailored solutions and insights that align with the lead's needs and interests. Email marketing is a powerful tool in this process, allowing for personalized communication that keeps your brand top of mind. Similarly, retargeting campaigns reminding leads of their interest through strategically placed ads across the web act as subtle nudges, encouraging them further down the funnel. Each interaction is meticulously designed to build trust, establish authority, and gradually overcome any reservations, moving the lead closer to the decision-making stage.

Conversion, the critical act of turning a lead into a customer, demands a blend of incentive and ease. Personalized offers, tailored to the preferences and past interactions of the lead, can tip the scales, transforming consideration into action. These offers, whether they be discounts, exclusive content, or personalized recommendations, should feel like a natural culmination of the nurturing process, a reward for the journey thus far. Equally important is ensuring a seamless buying experience—every step, from selecting a product to completing the purchase, should be frictionless. Simplifying the checkout process, offering multiple payment options, and providing clear, concise product information all contribute to removing barriers and making the path to purchase as straightforward as possible.

Successfully using the sales funnel requires recognizing that each lead's journey is unique despite the funnel's consistent structure. Embracing flexibility, understanding your audience's specific needs, and empathizing with potential customers is essential for guiding them from initial awareness to making a purchase.

## Customer Service Excellence: Building Loyalty

In the business world, the interactions between a brand and its customers form the core of their relationship. Among these interactions, customer service stands out as essential, with its power to lift a brand to greater levels of loyalty and respect. True exceptional customer service aims to exceed expectations, making each customer interaction a chance to strengthen their connection with the brand. This section dives into the key principles and strategies that transform customer service into an effective tool for gaining loyalty.

At the base of memorable customer service are principles that are the foundation for every interaction. These include empathy, responsiveness, personalization, and consistency. Empathy allows for a deeper understanding of the customer's needs and concerns, fostering a connection that is above transactional. Responsiveness ensures that queries and issues are addressed promptly, signaling to customers that their time and concerns are valued. Personalization tailors the service experience to the individual, making them feel recognized and appreciated. Consistency reassures customers of the reliability and quality of your service, regardless of the channel or touchpoint.

Gathering feedback from customers is needed to steer service improvements and spark innovation. This feedback can be collected through a variety of means, including surveys, social media interactions, and direct dialogue. Each method provides valuable insights, offering a well-rounded view of the customer experience. With their targeted questions, surveys help identify specific areas of satisfaction and improvement. Social media platforms provide open and honest feedback, giving you a glimpse into how the public views your brand. Direct interactions, whether face-to-face or through customer support avenues, add depth and context, enabling a more detailed understanding of customer views.

Extracting valuable insights from customer feedback requires careful analysis, where you dive into the data to spot trends, outliers, and areas for improvement. This process should evaluate both numerical data, like satisfaction scores, and narrative feedback, such as comments and suggestions. Utilizing advanced tools and approaches, such as sentiment analysis, determining the tone of feedback, and trend identification, can transform this data into practical insights. These insights can then inform your decision-making process, guiding actions that enhance your services and improve the overall customer experience.

Prioritizing and implementing changes based on customer feedback is a delicate balancing act, requiring a blend of strategic vision and operational pragmatism. It involves identifying initiatives that will have the most significant impact on customer satisfaction and loyalty and aligning them with business goals and resources. This process also entails setting clear objectives, timelines, and metrics for success, ensuring that each change is not just a reaction but a step toward a more customer-centric business model.

Communication plays a pivotal role in closing the feedback loop, signaling to customers that their input has been heard and acted upon. This involves transparently sharing the insights gathered and the steps taken in response, fostering a sense of collaboration and co-creation. Such communication can be woven into various touchpoints, from newsletters and social media updates to personalized messages, reinforcing the customer's role as a valued partner in the brand's evolution.

Focusing on customer retention is a practical application of the principle that it's less expensive to keep current customers than to find new ones. Strategies for retention revolve around frequent interaction, outstanding service, and the continuous provision of value, which together build a cycle of satisfaction that encourages loyalty and ongoing patronage. This approach increases the value customers bring over their lifetime and turns them into advocates for your brand, expanding your influence through their personal recommendations.

One way to build customer retention is a well-designed loyalty program that rewards and incentivizes repeat engagement, creating a stronger bond between the brand and its customers. The key is to offer rewards that are both desirable to the customer and sustainable for the business, from discounts and exclusive access to personalized offers. Such programs should also be easy to understand and participate in, ensuring they add value without complexity.

Utilizing customer data to tailor experiences adds a layer of depth and relevance to interactions, making customers feel uniquely seen and valued. This personalization can manifest in various forms, from customized product recommendations to targeted communication, each touchpoint carefully crafted to resonate with the individual's preferences and history with the brand.

The transformation of satisfied customers into vocal advocates for your brand is the ultimate accolade in customer service excellence. Encouraging this transition involves delivering consistently exceptional service and creating avenues for customers to share their experiences. This could include referral programs that reward customers for introducing friends and family or harnessing user-generated content to showcase real stories and testimonials.

Exceptional customer service sets a brand apart in the competitive business landscape, acting as a powerful draw for customers and encouraging their loyalty. This chapter has explored essential principles and strategies for transcending standard service expectations, laying the groundwork for a standout brand. By applying these insights, businesses can achieve operational excellence, transforming every customer interaction into a chance to strengthen connections and enhance their brand's stature.

# Chapter Seven

# Setting Up Day-to-Day Operations for Success

In this chapter, we dive into the practical steps of turning ideas into reality by setting up your workspace, a key factor in innovation, productivity, and growth. We'll look at how aligning your environment with your goals can lead to success, creating spaces supporting your business needs while fostering creativity and well-being. We'll explore the essentials of workspace optimization, focusing on efficiency, ergonomics, and technology and how to adapt these as your business grows.

## Setting Up Your Workspace

Creating an efficient workspace is about more than just good looks; it's about setting up your space in a way that makes work flow smoothly and productively. Picture a professional chef's kitchen where everything is within easy reach and ingredients are perfectly organized for quick use during the heat of cooking. In the same way, whether you're setting up a lively retail space or a peaceful home office, you need a setup that reduces interruptions and promotes fluid movement. This means placing your equipment thoughtfully, organizing storage smartly, and arranging your work areas in a way that lets tasks transition smoothly from one to the next.

This is a checklist for evaluating and enhancing workspace efficiency, covering everything from furniture arrangement to storage solutions, ensuring every element of your space contributes to a streamlined workflow.

**Workspace Efficiency Checklist**

- Furniture and Layout

- Lighting and Ventilation

- Technology and Equipment

- Storage Solutions

- Communication and Collaboration

- Health and Well-being

- Safety and Accessibility

- Aesthetics and Personal Touches

The science of ergonomics, which focuses on optimizing the interaction between people and their environments, plays a critical role in workspace design. A well-considered ergonomic setup minimizes the risk of strain and injury and elevates comfort, fostering an environment where extended periods of focus and creativity become possible and pleasurable. Consider the impact of a chair that supports the curve of the spine or a desk that positions your screen at eye level, small adjustments that can significantly enhance comfort and, by extension, performance.

In today's digital age, integrating technology and equipment into the workspace is not optional but imperative. The selection of these tools requires careful consideration and a balance between cutting-edge capabilities and practical necessity. For instance, a graphic design firm might invest in high-resolution monitors and advanced drawing tablets to bring creative visions to life, while a consultancy may prioritize robust video conferencing tools to connect with clients across the globe. The key lies in identifying the technologies that streamline operations and align with the specific demands of your work, ensuring that every tool enhances rather than encumbers your productivity.

The only constant in the journey of a business is change, a gradual scaling that might necessitate the expansion or optimization of your workspace. This evolution requires foresight and a flexible design that accommodates growth without necessitating a complete overhaul. Modular furniture, scalable technology solutions, and versatile storage systems offer a foundation that can evolve alongside your business. For instance, a start-up might choose desks that can easily be reconfigured into collaborative spaces or opt for cloud-based software that scales effortlessly with the addition of new team members. Anticipating growth in your workspace design ensures that your environment remains conducive to productivity, creativity, and well-being, regardless of the size or scope of your operations.

In crafting a workspace, whether it's transforming a corner in your home into a productivity haven or the meticulous design of a retail space that welcomes customers and inspires employees, the principles of efficiency, ergonomics, technology integration, and adaptability serve as your guide. Through this deliberate orchestration of space and function, your workspace becomes more than just a place of business—it evolves into a crucible of innovation, a sanctuary of creativity, and a testament to the journey from concept to creation.

## Essential Tools and Software for Your Business

In today's digital era, choosing and using the right digital tools and software is crucial for a business's success and flexibility. This section will navigate the digital transformation journey, showing how everything from cloud storage to project management software can improve operations, boost productivity, and strengthen your business's digital foundation.

Central to improving operations is the undeniable role of digital tools. This includes everything from cloud storage, easy access to data everywhere, and project management software, which accurately manages tasks. Digital transformation is more than just using new tools; it's about completely rethinking how business processes work. It's about using digital technology to make workflows more efficient, improve data analysis, and enable teamwork that isn't limited by location.

Choosing the right software for your business requires careful planning and a strategic mindset. With the vast options available, effectively choosing the right option for your business is essential. It's crucial to have a clear set of criteria that helps filter through the noise, pinpointing the tools that best match your business's needs and future goals. When selecting software, consider four key areas: functionality, adaptability, compatibility, and affordability. The software should not only meet your current requirements but also have the capacity to grow with your business. Its adaptability ensures it can scale up as your operations expand. Compatibility is about how well the software integrates with your existing systems, promoting a unified workflow and preventing data fragmentation. Lastly, while cost is always an important consideration, balancing it with the software's value in driving your business forward is essential, ensuring that your investment pays off in increased efficiency and growth potential.

The toolkit of vital software for today's businesses includes various applications, each designed to fulfill specific operational needs. Accounting software, for instance, is crucial for financial oversight, offering precision and ensuring regulatory compliance. Customer Relationship Management (CRM) systems are pivotal in connecting your business with its customers, gathering valuable insights to tailor interactions and inform sales tactics. For project oversight, management tools are indispensable, enabling the tracking of progress, allocation of tasks, and adherence to deadlines, thus promoting efficiency and responsibility. Additionally, inventory management software offers a live view of stock levels, optimizing the supply chain process and reducing the risks associated with excess inventory or stock shortages.

When considering software tools, consider automation. Automation in daily operations transforms the landscape of efficiency, taking it to new heights. To harness this power, examine everyday tasks and identify those that take up too much time or resources without requiring specialized skills. Automation tools streamline these tasks and make them effortless parts of your workflow. These range from email marketing platforms that send tailored messages to large groups of customers to scheduling tools that optimize resource distribution. The beauty of automation is its capacity to liberate your team from repetitive tasks, allowing them to concentrate on strategic planning and innovation.

In the fast-paced world of technology, keep up with the latest trends and tools to maintain a competitive edge. This ongoing quest for knowledge is key to ensuring your business stays ahead, using new technologies to enhance efficiency, spark innovation, and gain a competitive advantage. Staying technologically vigilant means more than just watching from the sidelines; it involves active participation, from engaging in industry discussions to trying out new tools that could revolutionize how you operate. By embracing a culture of continuous learning and adaptability, your business can stay agile, turning potential challenges into opportunities for growth and creativity.

## Hiring Your First Employee: When and How

Identifying when your business transitions from a solo project to a team effort is a key milestone in its development. This change, sometimes gradual, is signaled by an increasing workload and the complex mix of skills needed to bring your vision to life. Deciding to hire your first employee is a significant step because it reflects your business's growth and the crucial role of delegation and trust in effective leadership.

Deciding when to hire help is a critical turning point in your business's growth. It's like recognizing that your business, much like a complex machine, operates best with more hands on deck. This moment may arrive when you're missing out on opportunities because you're stretched too thin or when tasks that aren't your strong suit start accumulating. This decision is usually driven by the realization that the benefits of hiring—enhanced productivity, innovation, and increased revenue—far outweigh the cost of a new salary.

The process begins with a deep dive into the operational core of your business, identifying the areas where support is needed and could promote transformation. Whether it's the intricacies of digital marketing, the precision of financial management, or the creativity of product development, each domain holds the potential for exponential growth when tended by specialized hands.

Starting the hiring process is where your preparation and vision shape the outcome. The initial step is clearly defining the role you want to fill. This definition outlines the necessary skills, experiences, and personal qualities the job demands. It forms the basis of the job description, a document that not only spells out the role's duties and expectations but also reflects your company's values, drawing in applicants who align with your vision and culture.

The recruitment phase unfolds as a strategic campaign, utilizing platforms such as professional networks, job boards, and social media to broadcast your hiring needs. This stage requires consideration beyond just skill, so seek candidates with the potential to evolve and drive your business forward.

Interviews are the cornerstone of the hiring process, functioning not as a one-sided inquiry but as a mutual exploration. This phase is critical for assessing whether there is a match between the candidate's goals and the company's direction, a synergy of skills, and a compatibility of personalities. It's about determining a fit that elevates the relationship beyond mere employment to a collaborative partnership poised for collective achievement.

Making an offer, then, is a gesture that signifies trust and the promise of collaborative growth. It's a moment that solidifies the transition from a solo endeavor to a team-driven journey.

Welcoming a new employee into your business is like introducing a fresh element into a well-oiled machine. The onboarding process plays a vital role, aiming not only to acquaint the newcomer with day-to-day operations but also to integrate them into your company's unique culture and vision. This stage focuses more on building relationships, linking new hires with their team members, aligning them with their tasks, and connecting them to the company's overall objectives.

Effective onboarding strategies recommend a balanced methodology, blending structured orientations with casual interactions to foster a welcoming atmosphere. Implementing mentorship initiatives is highly beneficial, as they connect new hires with experienced colleagues who offer guidance, support, and a warm introduction to the company culture.

Continuous feedback loops, constructed through regular check-ins and open lines of communication, ensure that any hurdles in adaptation are promptly addressed, smoothing the transition and reinforcing the newcomer's confidence in their role and value to the team. When executed with care and intention, this process accelerates productivity and sets the foundation of loyalty and commitment.

In the evolution of your business, bringing on a new team member signifies both an accomplishment and a venture into the complexities of teamwork. This essential phase of hiring and onboarding represents a chance to foster new talent, cultivate an environment for innovation, and unite efforts toward shared objectives. Through thoughtful execution, this transition reshapes your business from an individual venture to a synergistic team, paving the way for future successes and opportunities.

## Outsourcing: What Tasks to Hand Off

In the process of growing a business, it's essential to recognize when it's more effective to delegate tasks to external entities rather than managing them in-house. Outsourcing isn't about relinquishing control but rather about strategically leveraging outside expertise to enhance your team's efficiency. This approach reflects the reality that today's businesses require a variety of skills, often beyond the capabilities of the current team, necessitating partnerships with external specialists.

Identifying which tasks to outsource requires a deep dive into your business operations to understand where your strengths lie and where you could use some help. Look for tasks that are critical but not necessarily central to your main business goals. For example, web development requires both technical know-how and creative insight, which may be outside your team's skill set. Content creation, essential for keeping your audience engaged, can quickly drain your internal resources, making it a strong candidate for outsourcing. Similarly, bookkeeping, although fundamental, involves meticulous attention to detail and adherence to regulations and might be more efficiently handled by external experts.

Choosing the right outsourcing partners is crucial, as their performance can significantly impact the outcome of your projects. At the core of this decision is the trust in their timely delivery and ability to meet or surpass your quality standards. Building this trust involves thorough research, including examining their past work and reading client reviews. However, it's not just about their skills or past achievements; it's also about how well their values and communication align with yours. These softer aspects can greatly influence the success and fluidity of your collaboration. Trying out a small pilot project with potential partners can be an effective way to test the waters, giving you a clearer view of how well you can work together in the long run.

Ensuring the quality of outsourced work is essential and demands a careful approach centered on open communication and agreed-upon terms. The key is clearly defining what you expect, not just in final outcomes but also in the finer details that signify true quality. Consistent communication creates a strong partnership through regular updates and feedback, ensuring the project stays true to your business's vision and quality standards. This continuous exchange, enhanced by technologies that track progress transparently, reduces the chance of misunderstandings and builds a relationship based on mutual respect and shared goals.

Outsourcing is a strategic move toward achieving excellence. This approach recognizes the finite nature of our resources and the vast opportunities that specialization offers. By carefully choosing tasks to outsource, ensuring high standards through diligent oversight, and maintaining transparent communication, outsourcing becomes a cornerstone strategy. It supports the growth and development of a business and enhances its capacity for innovation and impact.

## Supply Chain Management for Small Businesses

In the day-to-day operation of a small business, managing your supply chain is key. Think of it as the backbone that supports the flow of goods from start to finish. This network, which involves buying materials, making products, and getting them to customers, is complex. It requires careful planning and a deep understanding of how each part connects. Essentially, supply chain management is about ensuring products move smoothly from your suppliers to your customers. This smooth movement is vital for ensuring products are available when needed, of good quality, and cost-effective. It involves a careful balance, ensuring each step in the process is aligned with the market's changing needs.

Understanding the basics of supply chain management is crucial. It's about recognizing how every piece of the puzzle, from the raw materials to the final product, must fit perfectly together. Each element must reach its destination on time and in perfect condition. This careful coordination does more than just ensure your products are available; it also helps control costs, giving small businesses a fighting chance in a competitive market where thin margins make a big difference. Quick, reliable delivery is key to keeping customers happy and can turn the challenge of managing a supply chain into a significant advantage for your business.

Establishing strong relationships with suppliers is crucial to effectively managing your supply chain. By forming partnerships based on mutual benefits and trust, you lay the groundwork for ensuring the high quality and reliability of your products. Treating suppliers as integral to your business's objectives encourages a cooperative atmosphere, leading to open communication and shared ambitions that drive innovation and enhancements. Negotiating favorable terms with suppliers is not solely about reducing costs; it's a strategic move to boost your supply chain's flexibility and resilience. Holding regular meetings, openly sharing future plans, and working together to solve problems are key practices that reinforce these partnerships. Such efforts transform suppliers from mere vendors into valuable allies, fundamental to your business's success.

In inventory management, accuracy and forward planning are important. Achieving the right balance to avoid both excessive stock, which can immobilize your capital, and insufficient stock, which can lead to missed sales opportunities, demands a thoughtful strategy. Just-in-time inventory methods, which synchronize supplier orders with your production timelines and sales predictions, help reduce storage costs while ensuring products are available when needed. Adopting inventory management software provides instant visibility into your stock levels, enabling informed decisions that improve stock turnover and minimize excess. By taking this proactive approach, small businesses can save on resources and quickly adapt to changes in the market, ensuring they stay competitive in the dynamic business landscape.

Mitigating supply chain risks requires proactive and strategic planning. Diversifying your supplier base is crucial, as it reduces dependency on a single source and minimizes potential disruptions. Explore relationships with multiple suppliers for essential components and consider alternative materials or production methods for greater flexibility. Maintaining a safety stock, or a surplus inventory, is a buffer against unforeseen delays or demand spikes, safeguarding your operations. Regular audits and risk assessments of your supply chain identify vulnerabilities, allowing for timely adjustments. Embrace foresight and adaptability as key strategies to navigate the complexities of supply chains effectively.

## Creating a Culture of Innovation and Growth

In the business world, what sets a groundbreaking company apart from the rest is its culture. A culture focused on innovation and growth can propel a business to new heights, making it more adaptable and competitive. This mindset becomes the organization's driving force, encouraging creativity, building resilience, and fostering innovative ideas that push boundaries and challenge the norm.

Cultivating a culture of innovation and growth goes beyond simply wishing for it; it requires a proactive approach and thoughtful actions aimed at sparking, nurturing, and embedding innovation at all organizational levels. Motivating the team to embrace creativity is crucial. This means establishing physical and conceptual environments where ideas can emerge and thrive, unhampered by the fear of judgment or failure. Regular brainstorming sessions evolve into spaces where even the most unconventional ideas are encouraged, fostering the roots of innovation. Challenges framed as competitions or team projects ignite a spirit of rivalry and collaboration, prompting teams to exceed their expectations. Acknowledging and celebrating new ideas affirms the individual's role and demonstrates the organization's dedication to innovation, spurring an ongoing influx of new insights and approaches.

At the heart of this cultural framework lies the crucial role of a growth mindset, the belief that skills and intelligence can expand through effort and perseverance. This perspective forms the foundation for resilience, cultivating a space where obstacles are seen as paths to learning and development and where setbacks are considered valuable lessons rather than defeats. To embed this mindset throughout the organization, it's essential to foster a culture of continuous improvement, welcome constructive criticism, and celebrate every step forward, no matter how small.

Maintaining a thriving culture of innovation and growth demands consistent evaluation and flexibility. It is essential to define key metrics that embody the organization's innovative ethos, from the number of new ideas generated to the success rate of their implementation. Surveys and feedback mechanisms are effective tools for gauging employee perceptions of the company's commitment to innovation and personal growth. These strategies offer a snapshot of the current innovative climate and equip leaders with the necessary data to refine and bolster a culture of perpetual innovation.

In conclusion, envision your business as a dynamic force that's alive with innovation and growth. Its foundation is rooted in flexibility and an unwavering commitment to new prospects. At its core, your business is a catalyst for refining ideas, surmounting challenges, and intentionally shaping the future. This environment not only ensures survival but also enables your business to make a significant impact on its industry, turning challenges into opportunities and goals into realities. As we shift focus toward broader growth and expansion, the ethos of innovation and growth continues to guide us toward sustained success.

# Chapter Eight

## Scaling Your Business

### Growth Strategies: When and How to Scale

Identifying the perfect timing for expanding your business is fundamental. Imagine a farmer deciding when to plant seeds by carefully observing the soil's condition and the timing within the season to ensure the best harvest. Similarly, a business must look for specific signs indicating it's ready to grow. These signs include a steady increase in customer demand that surpasses what your current operations can handle, a solid financial base that doesn't rely on immediate external financing, and a competent workforce capable of adapting to growth. When these elements align, creating a ripe environment for growth, it's the prime time to consider taking your business to the next level.

Starting to scale your business without a strategic plan is like trying to steer a ship with no compass. Think of strategic planning as your guide, beginning by setting clear, measurable goals. Visualize where you want your business to be in one year, five years, or even ten years from now. These goals help you craft a roadmap that guides every decision, from recruiting new team members to innovating your product line. However, it's crucial that your roadmap remains adaptable. Just as a sailor adjusts to the shifting winds, pivoting and tackling unexpected challenges is key to navigating the complexities of business growth.

While often used interchangeably, scaling and growth encapsulate distinct concepts in the business realm. Growth implies adding resources at the same rate that revenue increases, a linear progression. Scaling, however, is about boosting revenue at a significantly faster rate than costs. Consider a software company that develops an app—once created, selling it to ten customers or 10,000 incurs no significant additional cost. This efficiency, doing more with less, is the essence of scaling, a balance that pivots on innovation and optimization.

Scaling introduces a new set of hurdles. Maintaining the quality of your product or service while reaching more customers, preserving the company culture that was perhaps easier to manage when the team was smaller, and ensuring systems and processes are robust enough to withstand increased operational demands are common challenges. For instance, a rapidly expanding restaurant might struggle to maintain the quality of dishes that made it popular initially. Overcoming these challenges requires a proactive approach, from investing in training and development to enhance team capabilities to implementing scalable systems that can support growth without compromising on the core values and quality that define your brand.

Scaling a business is a testament to its success, yet it demands a thoughtful approach that balances ambition with practicality. Recognizing the right moment to scale, planning strategically, understanding the difference between growth and scaling, and being prepared to face the challenges of expansion are crucial steps in this process. With the right preparation and mindset, scaling becomes not just a goal but a sustainable reality, marking the next chapter in your business's success story.

## Expanding Your Product Line

In today's ever-changing market, expanding your product range is more than just a strategy—it's a vital step for adapting to ever-changing customer needs and economic conditions. Think of it like a forest increasing its variety of plants to protect against diseases and wildfires; this approach in business helps spread risk over a wider selection of products or services and opens up new opportunities for revenue, breathing new life into your company.

The journey toward diversification begins with an in-depth analysis of market trends and a meticulous review that seeks to understand the current landscape and anticipate future shifts. This forward-looking perspective ensures that the expansion of the product line is not a reactionary measure but a proactive step toward capturing emerging market opportunities. Furthermore, engaging with the customer base through surveys, focus groups, and feedback mechanisms provides invaluable insights into unmet needs and desires, shaping the development of new offerings that resonate deeply with the target audience.

Leveraging existing capabilities presents a logical pathway for product line expansion. It entails an introspective examination of the business's current resources, from manufacturing processes to expertise, identifying areas where these strengths can be applied to new products or services. This approach not only capitalizes on the established proficiency and infrastructure but also ensures a level of familiarity and efficiency in the venture into new territories. For instance, a company specializing in artisanal chocolates might explore the creation of gourmet baking mixes, utilizing its expertise in flavor composition and its established supply chain for ingredients.

As your product line grows, it's crucial to keep a balance between your original offerings and new ones. This balance helps ensure that your brand's expansion strengthens rather than dilutes its identity and the quality your customers expect. Achieving this requires strategically managing resources to support both new and existing products effectively. Regularly evaluating this balance, with insights from customer feedback and performance data, is essential. This approach allows both core and new products to complement and enhance each other, maintaining the brand's integrity and fostering growth.

The strategic diversification journey is exemplified by businesses that have effectively widened their range of products, achieving significant growth milestones along the way.

A technology company that, starting with a singular focus on personal computers, branched out into mobile devices, wearable technology, and digital services. This expansion was not a departure from its core but an extension of its mission to innovate and enhance connectivity. Each new product, while distinct, carried the hallmark of quality and ingenuity, reinforcing the brand's position in the market and its relationship with consumers.

A small coffee roastery that, recognizing the burgeoning interest in home brewing, introduced a line of premium, sustainably sourced beans alongside brewing equipment and tutorials. This expansion catered to the evolving interests of its clientele, deepening engagement with the brand while opening new revenue channels.

These case studies showcase how understanding market trends, engaging with customers, and smartly allocating resources contribute to successful product line diversification. They highlight the need for careful planning that aligns new products with the brand's core identity and mission. By doing so, businesses can turn diversification from just a growth strategy into a source of resilience and long-term relevance in a constantly changing market.

## Exploring New Markets: Expansion Strategies

Identifying suitable opportunities for business expansion requires comprehensive market research. This involves charting new territories using both quantitative data, like statistics, and qualitative insights, such as customer feedback. Utilizing tools such as surveys, interviews, and competitor analysis can uncover customer desires, behaviors, and market gaps. Additionally, examining broader trends and economic factors can highlight growing sectors and emerging opportunities. By integrating these insights, your expansion decisions become well-informed and reality-based, moving beyond speculation.

Selecting the best path for expanding your market requires carefully analyzing different growth models, each offering its own set of benefits and obstacles. Expanding geographically, whether it's to neighboring areas or across the globe, opens up new market possibilities. However, it's essential to grasp the cultural nuances and navigate the regulatory environments of these new areas. On the other hand, demographic diversification focuses on reaching new customer groups within already existing markets, allowing for a deeper market presence with less logistical complexity. Yet, this approach depends heavily on precisely targeted marketing efforts. The digital landscape presents a limitless marketplace where businesses can surpass geographical boundaries through online platforms. This digital expansion demands a strong grasp of digital marketing and robust cybersecurity protocols. The key to successful expansion lies in matching your business's strategic objectives with its operational strengths, ensuring that your chosen growth model reaches new markets and complements your brand's core values and vision.

Seeking new markets often leads to the formation of strategic partnerships, acting as both a shortcut to valuable local knowledge and a solid base for ongoing growth. By forming alliances with local distributors, who bring their established networks and deep understanding of the market, or by creating joint ventures that pool resources and expertise for shared success, these partnerships can significantly extend a brand's reach while reducing risks. The success of such partnerships hinges on having aligned goals, clear and open communication, and a mutual dedication to maintaining quality and integrity. Much like an orchestra where each member contributes their unique sound yet plays in unison, these collaborative efforts flourish when there's a unity of purpose and mutual respect.

While venturing into new markets, you'll encounter challenges such as logistical hurdles and fierce competition. Overcoming these obstacles requires resilience, adaptability, and strategic foresight. Addressing logistical issues might involve re-thinking your supply chain or embracing local manufacturing practices to improve efficiency and flexibility. Customizing your products and marketing strategies to reflect local languages and cultural practices can increase your brand's appeal and accessibility to new audiences. Moreover, gaining a competitive advantage demands a comprehensive understanding of the competitive landscape, leveraging your unique selling points, and fostering continuous innovation. Throughout this process, main-taining a laser focus on the needs and feedback of your customers is paramount. This focus acts as a guide, helping you make informed adjustments and ensuring your brand remains relevant and competitive amid the ever-changing market dynamics.

***

**Success Story:** One notable success story in market expansion is the global coffee giant, Starbucks. Starting as a single store in Seattle in 1971, Starbucks leveraged a strategic approach to market expansion that fueled its rise into a multinational brand.

**Starbucks' Market Expansion Strategy**

1. Gradual Domestic Expansion: Starbucks initially focused on expanding its footprint across the United States. The company adopted a cluster strategy, opening stores in close proximity within the same neighborhood to increase brand visibility and market saturation before moving on to a new region.

2. International Expansion: After establishing a strong domestic presence, Starbucks began its international expansion in the mid-1990s. It carefully selected international markets that valued premium brands and coffee culture. Its first overseas location in

Tokyo, Japan, opened in 1996, which proved a significant success and paved the way for expansion across Asia and beyond.

3. Local Adaptation Strategy: A key to Starbucks' successful expansion has been its ability to adapt to local cultures while maintaining its brand identity. It offers menu items catering to local tastes and preferences in different regions. For example, in China, Starbucks introduced tea-based beverages and locally popular mooncakes.

4. Strategic Partnerships and Alliances: Starbucks often entered new markets through joint ventures or licensing arrangements with local companies that had strong market knowledge. This approach helped mitigate risks associated with entering unfamiliar markets.

5. Emphasis on Store Atmosphere and Location: Starbucks stores are strategically located in high-traffic, high-visibility settings in each new market. The company ensures that its stores reflect the character and culture of the neighborhood, which enhances local customer acceptance.

**Outcome of Expansion**

This strategic approach has proven remarkably successful. As of 2021, Starbucks operates over 32,000 stores across 80 countries. Its international ventures account for a significant portion of its revenue, demonstrating effective market penetration and brand acceptance globally.

***

The business world abounds with tales of brands that have successfully navigated new markets, from tech giants transforming into household names to niche brands achieving global recognition by tapping into universal themes or offering distinct products. These success stories offer both inspiration and invaluable lessons, highlighting key strategies such as understanding target markets, forming strategic partnerships, and consistently upholding brand integrity and customer satisfaction. By examining these examples, businesses can glean practical insights and strategies, offering a roadmap for successful market expansion.

## Exit Strategies: Knowing When and How to Move On

In the lifecycle of every business, moments arrive when the path ahead forks, presenting options that lead toward distinct horizons. Among these, the consideration of an exit strategy emerges not as an admission of defeat or a signal of the end but as a strategic pivot toward new beginnings or transformations. This foresight into the eventual transition of business ownership or structure is as integral to the planning process as the initial blueprint of the business itself. It acknowledges the fluid nature of markets, personal goals, and life itself, allowing for graceful transitions that preserve legacy and value.

The landscape of exit strategies is diverse and multifaceted, offering various pathways to draw a business journey to a close or transform its direction. One popular route is selling the business, which rewards years of hard work with financial returns. In this scenario, the business you've painstakingly built becomes a lasting legacy, a symbol of your entrepreneurial journey. Another option is passing the business on to family members, ensuring its legacy continues under the guidance of those who share its core values and vision. For those looking beyond, initiating an Initial Public Offering (IPO) can provide the business with fresh capital, broadening its scope and influence. These exit paths each come with their own set of considerations, hurdles, and potential rewards, requiring thorough planning and reflection.

Preparing your business for an exit, whether through sale or another route, is like preparing a flight for takeoff, ensuring it's ready and valuable. This involves several steps, including organizing financial records and demonstrating the business's profitability and growth potential. Making operations more efficient and improving or expanding strategically makes your business more appealing to potential buyers or investors. This often requires looking at your business from an outsider's perspective to spotlight strengths and improve on any weaknesses.

Embarking on the exit journey is like running through a maze of negotiations, financial assessments, and legal complexities, each phase demanding precision and strategic thinking. The business valuation is the pivotal first step, a detailed analysis that evaluates tangible assets, financial health, market standing, brand reputation, and future growth prospects. Identifying an ideal buyer or investor that meets financial expectations and aligns with the business's vision requires a blend of patience and keen judgment. The negotiation phase is a fine-tuned balancing act where dreams meet reality and ambition meets practicality. The subsequent transition, whether transferring ownership, merging with a larger entity, or transitioning to public ownership, calls for thorough planning to ensure a smooth changeover for employees, clients, and stakeholders. Though fraught with challenges, this phase presents a unique chance to honor the business's legacy and celebrate the hard work invested.

Exploring exit strategies reveals the core of entrepreneurship, a journey marked by beginnings, growth, and strategic evolution. This chapter highlights how exit strategies are not finalities but pivotal shifts toward new opportunities for growth, innovation, and personal evolution. It stresses the importance of viewing exit strategies as moments of transformation integral to the business lifecycle. A well-planned exit not only honors the business's legacy but also opens doors to future ventures, underscoring the dynamic nature of entrepreneurship.

# Chapter Nine

# Overcoming Common Entrepreneurial Challenges

Every entrepreneur carries a resilience that often remains hidden until adversity challenges them. This resilience shines brightest not during success but in the face of trials when obstacles appear insurmountable, and the future seems uncertain. These challenging moments truly define an entrepreneur—not the accomplishments highlighted by the media but the quiet determination to rise, dust oneself off, and continue moving forward. This chapter examines the journey through failure, a universal experience for entrepreneurs, yet one that leaves each individual changed in unique ways. We delve into how failures, though daunting, can be transformed into valuable lessons, navigating the complex path of setbacks with guidance derived from wisdom and lived experiences.

## Dealing with Failure: Lessons and Resilience

The stigma attached to failure in the business world is a mirage, a deceptive shadow obscuring the invaluable lessons in its wake. Like a seasoned gardener who understands that pruning is crucial for growth, embracing failure as an integral part of growth liberates one from the fear of falling short. Rejection and failure, far from being the antithesis of success, are its precursors, shaping the resilience and adaptability that characterize enduring enterprises. Reflecting on the countless inventors and pioneers who faced rejection multiple times before their breakthroughs, it becomes clear that the path to innovation is paved with setbacks. Each "no" brings one step closer to a "yes," each closed door a redirection toward the one that swings wide open.

Within the shadows of failure, invaluable lessons wait to be discovered by those eager to seek them out. This journey of learning from one's missteps mirrors the process of a scientist meticulously evaluating an experiment that didn't go as planned, not to assign blame but to gain clarity and insight. It requires a balanced review of the missteps, combined with the humility to own up to them and the resolve to do better. Highlighting businesses that successfully adapted after facing challenges, these stories underscore the notion that today's setbacks can become the cornerstones of tomorrow's success.

Resilience is not just an innate quality but also a skill that entrepreneurs develop over time, especially when faced with challenges. Building resilience involves a variety of strategies, from engaging in mindfulness to keep one's balance during difficult periods to establishing small, practical goals that help rebuild confidence step by step. Reflection helps redefine failure, shifting it from being a mark of defeat to a symbol of perseverance and growth. Through such practices, resilience becomes a cultivated strength, offering a way to navigate the complexities of business with grit and grace.

A support network is paramount to overcoming entrepreneurial hurdles. Entrepreneurs embedded within a network of mentors, peers, and supporters are less likely to stumble amidst challenges. Such a network provides emotional backing and practical insights, presenting viewpoints that might be overlooked in times of setbacks. Through initiatives like mastermind groups or entrepreneur circles, a collaborative environment is fostered where experiences and tactics are exchanged, and motivation is abundantly shared. This emphasizes that the entrepreneurial journey is not a solitary one. Participating in these face-to-face or digital communities serves as a crucial support system, offering guidance and stability when navigating tough times.

**Case Studies of Failure to Success**

Our case study involves a tech start-up that, upon launching its first product, faced critical software flaws that rendered it nearly obsolete. Instead of folding, the team conducted exhaustive customer feedback sessions, identifying the technical shortcomings and unmet needs that their initial model failed to address. This feedback became the blueprint for a revamped product that rectified the original issues and introduced innovative features that set it apart from competitors. The start-up's journey from a near-fatal launch to market leadership underscores the potency of resilience, the value of customer engagement, and the transformative power of failure.

***

Navigating the entrepreneurial journey, every business owner must accept failure as a possibility and an integral part of their path. This acceptance unveils failure's hidden value; it's an opportunity for growth, innovation, and resilience. Understanding that setbacks are not just hurdles but opportunities for learning, we can harness them to bolster our resolve, expand our support networks, and draw wisdom from those who've prevailed over similar challenges. This mindset transforms our approach to entrepreneurship, allowing us to view each setback not as a setback but as a vital step toward success.

## Dealing with Financial Hardships

Financial surprises can blindside you in the unpredictable world of starting and running a business, making an emergency fund an essential lifeline. Think of this fund not just as a safety net for unexpected expenses but also as a key tool that gives you the stability to steer through rough economic waters. Building this fund requires discipline and a strategic allocation of resources set aside for the times when the market becomes unstable. The goal here is not to be pessimistic but prepared. Having an emergency fund ensures that your business can survive sudden financial shocks, like a market downturn, unexpected costs, or a global economic crisis, without going under.

Achieving financial balance, especially in times of limited cash flow, highlights the importance of smart cost management. This effort requires careful and precise expense reduction that maintains the integrity and quality of your product or service, the core of your business. Effective strategies for this type of cost management include renegotiating contracts to secure better terms that reflect the current market or the benefits of long-term relationships. Simplifying operations, cutting unnecessary steps, and leveraging technology can also help lower costs. Moving toward a lean way of operating, focusing on flexibility and innovation rather than unnecessary expenses, ensures that every penny is spent in a way that adds real value to what you offer your customers.

In the midst of financial challenges, it's easy to feel overwhelmed. However, these moments are more than just obstacles; they're opportunities for growth and learning. By shifting our view of financial difficulties from problems to be feared to lessons to be learned, we can transform our approach to business. This process starts with carefully reviewing past financial decisions and pinpointing where things went wrong, whether it was overestimating how much people would want what you're selling, spending too much on running your business, or not keeping a close enough eye on your finances. This kind of reflection, along with a dedication to ongoing education, sharpens your financial skills. It improves your ability to manage money and strengthens your resilience in the face of future challenges. Seeking advice from financial experts, attending workshops, and using online resources to boost your financial knowledge can help turn previous financial setbacks into valuable lessons, laying the groundwork for a stronger, more informed approach to running your business.

## Time Management for Entrepreneurs: Finding Balance

In the fast-paced world of starting and running a business, every second counts as both a chance for growth and a call to action. Successfully managing time is not just a useful skill; it's essential for both your personal happiness and the success of your business. Finding a balance between the constant forward march of time and our limited personal energy requires a strategy that goes beyond simple scheduling. It involves creating a daily routine that prioritizes tasks, sets clear goals, and makes the most of every moment. As entrepreneurs, we're in control, navigating our businesses through urgent deadlines and less critical tasks while ensuring we also attend to our own needs. This balance is crucial for keeping the business moving forward without compromising our well-being.

At the core of effective time management lies the art of prioritization, a discerning eye that distinguishes the vital from the merely important, the urgent from the optional. The Eisenhower Matrix, a simple yet powerful tool, helps divide tasks into four quadrants based on their urgency and importance. This method helps in focusing on tasks that align with long-term objectives rather than getting caught up in day-to-day emergencies. By encouraging entrepreneurs to take a moment to think before acting, this approach promotes strategic decision-making over knee-jerk reactions, ensuring every step taken is in the direction of the ultimate business goals.

In the vast world of entrepreneurship, where the lines between work and life often blur, setting clear boundaries is key to maintaining both your productivity and personal well-being. These boundaries, though unseen, are crucial for protecting your personal time, ensuring you don't lose your identity to your business role. By clearly marking your work hours and committing to switch off during your personal time, you create a defense against burnout. This keeps your energy and passion for your business alive. Moreover, this deliberate separation helps you build healthier relationships, enabling you to be fully present in your personal life and making your leisure time truly rejuvenating.

Time management tools and apps are like secret weapons for entrepreneurs, helping turn chaos into clarity by organizing tasks and schedules efficiently. These digital assistants range from calendar apps that keep all your devices in sync to project management platforms that simplify complex tasks into doable steps. They keep things in order and streamline your workload. Think of them as your digital brain, storing your duties and dreams, allowing you to focus on the creative and critical thinking needed to drive your business forward. Choosing the right tools, customized to fit your unique business rhythm, makes planning precise. This ensures that every minute counts and every action is impactful, ensuring you're always moving closer to your goals.

Delegation emerges as a critical skill in the entrepreneurial journey, acting as a multiplier of your efforts. It's about identifying tasks others can perform, whether they're on your team or outside collaborators. More than just offloading work, strategic delegation recognizes your limits and harnesses the strengths of others. It's built on trust and empowerment, allowing you to focus on where your vision is most needed. Effective delegation depends on clear communication, setting explicit expectations, and providing necessary support. This boosts your productivity and fosters a culture of growth and accountability. In this environment, everyone's potential is maximized, propelling the team toward collective goals.

In the relentless journey toward entrepreneurial success, where time is precious and limited, the tactics of prioritizing, establishing boundaries, utilizing tools, and delegating are crucial. They navigate through challenges and obstacles, ensuring that despite ongoing demands and a fast pace, there's a continuous effort to maintain balance and safeguard personal well-being amidst a host of responsibilities. This balance is key to achieving genuine productivity, fueled by a sense of well-being and a clear goal that every moment invested is a step closer to fulfilling your greatest ambitions.

> **Action Step:** Fill out your weekly planner. Be sure to include personal time and days off.

## Overcoming Burnout

In the world of starting a business, every choice paves the future, yet the threat of burnout is ever-present, quietly trailing the enthusiasm of ambition. It doesn't strike in obvious moments of crisis but rather in the quiet periods of non-stop effort. Entrepreneurs, driven to build their dreams, often overlook the initial signs of fatigue, the quiet indicators that their reservoir of creativity and perseverance is running low. These signs—irritability, insomnia, and a feeling of aimlessness—are the body's way of signaling the need to slow down and reassess the demanding pace of entrepreneurship. Acknowledging these early warnings is crucial in protecting the entrepreneur's health and the health of their business. After all, the success of the venture is deeply intertwined with the founder's well-being.

The delicate balance between time spent on your business and personal life is crucial for every entrepreneur. This balance, often talked about but rarely achieved, is key to maintaining both productivity and creativity over the long term. The myth that success requires a complete surrender of one's time and energy to the business is just that, a myth. In reality, creating a healthy work-life balance is not a sign of a lack of dedication but a necessary strategy for long-term success. This involves drawing clear boundaries between work and personal time and learning to say no to external demands to protect your own energy and focus. Prioritizing tasks effectively ensures that important activities get the attention they deserve while less critical ones are set aside. Regular breaks are also essential, allowing both mind and body the time to rest and recharge, ready to tackle the next challenge.

Facing the constant pressure of starting a business, finding solace in stress management techniques is crucial. With its emphasis on staying present and engaged, mindfulness shines a light through the fog of mental clutter, bringing calm where there is turmoil. Engaging in regular physical exercise serves as an effective outlet for stress, clearing away feelings of tiredness and frustration. Equally important is maintaining a balanced diet—nutrition often takes a backseat amidst the hustle, but it's vital for keeping energy levels steady and bolstering resilience. These simple yet powerful strategies protect against stress's damaging effects and the ever-present risk of burnout.

At its core, self-care is about reclaiming your time and energy from the demands of running a business. It includes activities that refresh your soul and revive your mind, like engaging in physical exercise, practicing meditation, or enjoying hobbies. These moments, which may seem minor, are actually crucial for recharging and finding new inspiration. By aligning these practices with your personal interests and passions, they become more than just a way to prevent burnout; they celebrate your individuality and remind you there's a world outside your business.

Yet, self-care and stress management, for all their potency, are sometimes insufficient shields against the barrage of burnout. In these moments, when the weight becomes unbearable, seeking support transcends suggestion to become imperative. With their wisdom and experience, mentors offer guidance, a way to navigate through the fog with insights born of similar journeys. Peers provide solace, a shared understanding that one is not alone in the struggle. With their expertise, mental health professionals offer strategies to reclaim one's mental and emotional equilibrium. This circle of support, diverse in its composition, serves as a wall against the isolation that burnout provokes, a collective force that upholds the entrepreneur even as they falter.

In the entrepreneur's journey, encountering burnout is not a sign of weakness but rather a testament to their commitment and effort. Tackling this challenge involves not merely returning to a previous state but evolving to adopt a more resilient stance in both personal and professional realms. This requires ongoing attentiveness to personal needs alongside business demands. Striving for balance becomes a daily practice, where action meets reflection and innovation pairs with introspection, fostering growth in both the entrepreneur and their enterprise. Success, in this context, transcends business achievements by embodying the personal fulfillment and development encountered along the way.

> **Actions Step**: List your hobbies and what you will do during your personal time.

## Crisis Management: Keeping Your Business Alive

In today's ever-changing world, unpredictability is the norm, and businesses face numerous challenges and crises. To successfully steer through these difficult times, entrepreneurs need a plan that is both forward-thinking and adaptable, a strategy that prepares for potential problems while guiding the business safely through them. This approach doesn't only involve spotting possible dangers but also creating a detailed yet flexible action plan that ensures the business can continue, recover, and even grow stronger through adversity. By preparing carefully for every eventuality, businesses can protect themselves against potential crises, turning these challenges into opportunities for development and improvement.

Preparation for potential crises begins with the meticulous mapping of the landscape, an endeavor that extends beyond the horizon of immediate concerns to encompass a broad spectrum of eventualities. Risk assessment becomes the tool in this process, a systematic evaluation that identifies vulnerabilities, from operational disruptions to financial instability and environmental catastrophes. This assessment identifies the potential threats, allowing for the construction of a contingency plan that is both comprehensive and adaptable. Such detailed yet flexible plans outline the steps for immediate response and the pathways for sustained operation under duress. This ensures that the business remains afloat and proactive in the face of adversity.

In the midst of crisis-induced chaos, the role of clear and honest communication cannot be overstated. It acts as a guide for all stakeholders: leaders, employees, customers, and investors alike. The success of steering through crises hinges on how effectively a business communicates. Messages should be timely, transparent, and consistent, as they play a critical role in either building or destroying trust. Each communication reflects the business's dedication to integrity and responsibility. Therefore, crafting these messages requires a factual approach and a deep understanding and empathy for the audience's concerns and questions. It's essential that the information shared reaches its intended audience and connects with them, offering reassurance in times of uncertainty.

As the dust settles, revealing the altered landscape left in the wake of a crisis, the capacity to adapt becomes the entrepreneur's most valued asset. This adaptability, however, is not a mere reaction to change but a proactive transformation of business models, offerings, or operations that aligns with the new reality. It's a pivot that draws on the insights gleaned from the crisis, turning lessons learned into strategies implemented, ensuring that the business survives and thrives in the aftermath. This adaptation process may involve the diversification of supply chains to mitigate future disruptions, the digitalization of services to meet the demands of a remote customer base, or even a complete overhaul of the product lineup to address the shifting needs of the market. Each of these adjustments, guided by strategic foresight and innovative thinking, serves to realign the business with its environment, turning the scars of crisis into badges of resilience.

The aftermath of a crisis is filled with obstacles, each one an opportunity for recovery, rebuilding, and rejuvenation. This critical phase demands a comprehensive approach that transcends operational repair, tackling the psychological and emotional impact on stakeholders. Evaluating the crisis's effects goes beyond financial audits, diving into morale, brand perception, and customer loyalty. These insights guide the rebuilding process, transforming it into a chance for innovation. By incorporating the crisis's lessons into the business's core, companies can enhance efficiency, resilience, and agility. Rebuilding stakeholder confidence, whether employees or investors, requires showing tangible signs of renewal. This commitment to emerge stronger, more adaptable, and in tune with market demands fosters trust and solidifies the business's standing within its community.

Within a crisis's core, where pressures mount, and uncertainties grow, lies a potent chance for profound transformation. These testing times unveil an entrepreneur's resilience and the business's robustness. Through diligent preparation, transparent communication, strategic adjustments, and a commitment to recovery, businesses navigate crisis chaos effectively. They evolve from mere survivors to architects of their future, turning obstacles into opportunities for growth and disruptions into catalysts for innovation.

## Pivoting: When to Change Course

In the fluid dynamics of the market, recognizing the need for a pivot is like a sailor sensing a shift in the wind, necessitating a recalibration of sails to harness the new direction. For entrepreneurs, this acute awareness is pivotal; it's the ability to read the undercurrents of consumer behavior, technological evolution, and competitive landscapes. Signals that a pivot might be necessary can manifest as a plateau in growth, a consistent misalignment between product offerings and customer feedback, or an emerging technology rendering existing solutions obsolete. These subtle yet significant indicators suggest that the original course, while once promising, now requires adjustment to align with the evolving market topography.

Embarking on the pivot process is a delicate endeavor that demands a methodical approach that balances speed with deliberateness. It begins with a deep dive into market research, an expedition to unearth the nuances of consumer needs unmet by current offerings, and to identify emerging trends that signal opportunities for differentiation. This research acts as the compass guiding the pivot, ensuring that the new direction is not just a reaction to pressure but a strategic move toward greater alignment with market demands. Prototyping emerges as the next step—an experimentation phase where ideas transform into tangible models that are tested and iterated upon. This iterative process, fueled by real-world feedback, refines the pivot, sculpting it into a form that resonates with both existing customers and untapped markets. Throughout this journey, continuous engagement with the audience provides invaluable insights, turning feedback into the very clay from which the new business model or product is molded.

Managing stakeholder expectations during this time of transformation is a tightrope walk, requiring transparency, communication, and the nurturing of trust. For employees, the pivot may bring uncertainty and concern for the future direction of the company and their place within it. Addressing these concerns head-on, through open forums and regular updates, builds a culture of inclusivity, turning potential apprehension into collective enthusiasm for the new path. For investors and partners, the pivot presents a recalibration of risk and reward, necessitating a clear articulation of the rationale behind the shift, backed by data and a coherent strategy that outlines the path to renewed growth and profitability. In these conversations, honesty and clarity are the cornerstones, ensuring that stakeholders remain aligned, supportive, and engaged.

***

The chronicles of business history are filled with stories of successful pivots, serving as both guideposts and inspiration for those at pivotal moments in their journey.

Netflix, a prominent online streaming service, began as a DVD rental business, a pivot that was prescient in its anticipation of digital media's dominance.

Slack, a software company that shifted from a failed gaming platform to a globally dominant communications tool, illustrating the power of reimagining technology to meet broader needs.

These stories underscore a universal truth: that within the heart of change lies opportunity, not just for survival but for profound growth and innovation. The lessons gained from these pioneers are manifold, emphasizing the importance of agility, customer-centricity, and the courage to reimagine one's business in the face of evolving landscapes.

***

In navigating the complex terrain of entrepreneurship, the capacity to pivot—to realign one's course in response to the shifting winds of the market—is a testament to the enduring spirit of innovation that defines the entrepreneurial ethos. It's a recognition that the path to success is not linear but winding, filled with turns and detours that, while unexpected, lead to richer, more fertile ground. The pivot, then, becomes a strategic maneuver in the entrepreneur's repertoire, a bold stroke that underscores the adaptability and resilience necessary to thrive in the ever-changing business world.

As this exploration of the pivot concludes, it beckons entrepreneurs to embrace change not with trepidation but with anticipation, viewing each shift in the market as a canvas upon which new opportunities can be painted. This mindset, rooted in flexibility, innovation, and an unwavering focus on the customer, ensures that businesses remain relevant and ahead of the curve, turning the challenges of today into the triumphs of tomorrow. In this spirit, we move forward, ready to face the next chapter with the knowledge that in change lies the seed of growth and, in adaptability, the path to enduring success.

# Chapter Ten

# Maintaining Your Entrepreneurial Spirit

**Staying Motivated**

Motivation, the elusive spark that fuels the engine of progress, often dims under the weight of monotony or adversity. The key to reigniting it lies not in grand gestures but in the aggregation of small, deliberate actions, a series of kindlings that together can fan the flames back to life.

Entrepreneurs rely on their goals to set a direction and purpose. Our goals must evolve to stay aligned with our ambitions and what's realistically achievable. It's crucial to periodically review and adjust these targets, blending logic with passion to ensure our aims are both within reach and truly fulfilling. Consider scheduling regular goal-review sessions, perhaps at the beginning of each quarter, as a way to recalibrate and recommit to your entrepreneurial journey.

Inspiration, often found in the stories of others, reminds us that the path we tread has been navigated before. Attending industry events, where the air buzzes with the electricity of shared ambition, or joining an entrepreneurial community offers a wellspring of motivation. In the thrum of collective endeavor, personal trials are contextualized within a broader narrative of resilience and triumph. Such engagements also serve as informal benchmarks, opportunities to measure one's progress against the backdrop of the community's achievements and challenges.

Gratitude, the quiet acknowledgment of progress and privilege, grounds us. It's the antidote to the entrepreneur's perennial pursuit of more, a pause to breathe and behold how far the journey has come. Keeping a gratitude journal, a simple notebook where daily victories are recorded, transforms our perception. It shifts focus from what remains to be done to what has been accomplished, from the gap to the gain. This subtle shift in perspective is profound, breeding contentment and resilience in the face of adversity.

In a world that glorifies milestones, the power of small wins remains undervalued. Yet, it's these minor victories, the successful client meeting or the completion of a project phase, that accumulate into significant progress. Creating a culture that celebrates these achievements, perhaps with a team dinner or a personal reward like a day off, reinforces motivation. It converts the entrepreneurial marathon into a series of sprints, each with its finish line and its accolades, ensuring that motivation is continually renewed.

During quieter times, when external sources of motivation dry up, entrepreneurs must embark on self-reflection. In these moments, true resilience is tested, not just overcoming obstacles but also reigniting inner drive. This chapter equips entrepreneurs with strategies for this self-reflective journey, offering ways to maintain motivation independently. Through targeted actions, thoughtful reflection, and leveraging community support, entrepreneurs learn to keep their passion alive, ensuring their business thrives through both calm and challenging periods.

## Embracing Lifelong Learning: Resources and Practices

In the entrepreneurial journey, the constantly evolving business landscape demands more than relying on past achievements. Mental agility, developed through an ongoing commitment to learning, empowers an entrepreneur to navigate unpredictable market dynamics effectively. This dedication to acquiring knowledge isn't just another task on the to-do list; it's essential for survival and success, allowing entrepreneurs to adapt and thrive amidst the challenges and opportunities that the world of business presents.

Today's digital era is a treasure trove of knowledge, with a variety of online resources available at our fingertips. Websites like Coursera and Udemy open the door to a wide range of subjects, from the complexities of blockchain to digital marketing strategies, catering to those eager to learn. Additionally, webinars provide direct insights from industry pioneers, offering a real-time peek into the minds driving innovation. For those on the go, podcasts make it easy to turn every commute into a learning opportunity, discussing varied topics, including the culture of start-ups, methods for growth hacking, and leadership insights.

The journey to gain knowledge shouldn't be walked alone. Vibrant communities at networking events and online forums are crucial for exchanging ideas and real-world experiences. By engaging with peers and mentors, entrepreneurs uncover the practical truths behind starting and running a business, insights that go beyond what textbooks teach. These authentic interactions promote a culture of shared growth, enlightening the path for every entrepreneur.

At the core of every entrepreneur is a deep-seated curiosity, a drive for continuous learning that demands regular nurturing. This can be achieved by engaging with the broader business ecosystem. Actions such as subscribing to industry newsletters, following thought leaders on social media, and joining discussions on platforms like LinkedIn or Clubhouse are essential. They keep the entrepreneurial spirit ignited, ensuring curiosity serves as a beacon rather than diminishes in the market noise. Through this active engagement, hidden opportunities emerge, ready for the observant entrepreneur to discover and exploit.

Developing a learning plan requires careful planning, blending your dreams with what's practically achievable. This strategy isn't fixed but adapts over time, capturing both your learning goals and the steps to get there. It covers everything from picking up new skills that enhance your business capabilities to deepening your knowledge in areas you're already familiar with. Setting SMART learning objectives ensures your efforts are focused and purposeful. This plan is a dynamic document reflecting your dedication to ongoing growth, and it changes as you and your business evolve.

The entrepreneur's commitment to lifelong learning is their ultimate asset. This dedication enables adaptation and evolution and fosters growth beyond current limitations. This continuous quest for knowledge and unwavering curiosity drives entrepreneurs to navigate and lead in the ever-evolving business world. They don't just partake in the journey; they pioneer new paths, shaping the future of innovation and success.

## Fostering a Supportive Network

In the entrepreneurial journey, building a supportive network is crucial. This community, diverse in backgrounds and experiences, serves not just as a platform for brainstorming but as an essential support system during both challenging and successful times. Creating such a network requires deliberate effort to establish meaningful connections that foster growth and challenge comfort zones.

Starting a supportive community begins with an open heart and mind, ready to venture beyond individual efforts and embrace shared wisdom. It means stepping into the entrepreneurship ecosystem, where individuals with diverse insights, failures, and successes meet. Active participation in forums and events and a genuine curiosity about others' stories foster a space where meaningful connections can flourish. These connections, rooted in mutual respect and a shared entrepreneurial spirit, lay the groundwork for a network that encourages growth and innovation.

The transformation from initial connections to a strong support network is defined by developing deeper relationships through consistent interaction and commitment. This process involves going beyond basic conversations to unlock opportunities for collaboration, mentorship, and partnership. Cultivating these deeper bonds requires an environment of openness, where sharing vulnerabilities is as natural as celebrating successes, and generosity guides the exchange of knowledge and resources. In such a setting, trust thrives, creating a network that supports and elevates every member to their fullest potential.

Mastermind groups play a pivotal role in the ecosystem of support networks, acting as a unifying force that intertwines individual goals into a shared mission. Though small, these groups are impactful in their reach, uniting entrepreneurs of various backgrounds around a mutual dedication to growth and responsibility. Their meetings, marked by regularity and a clear agenda, facilitate the exchange of ideas, strategies, and experiences. In these gatherings, members set goals, track progress, and uphold accountability through a shared commitment rather than external pressures. The significance of these groups extends beyond the acquisition of practical advice to the transformative power of collective focus. This shared energy drives each entrepreneur toward their objectives and instills a sense of purpose and motivation across the group.

Seeking mentorship is embarking on a quest for wisdom, a venture into the realm of knowledge shaped by experience and challenges. Mentors, endowed with deep insights, provide advice and a broader perspective that lights the way forward. Finding a mentor is about finding a shared set of values, a connection that goes beyond simple knowledge transfer to resonate with one's motivations and goals. This mentor-mentee relationship thrives on reciprocity; it's not a one-directional flow of wisdom but a mutual exchange that benefits from the new energy and perspectives the mentee brings. This exchange is a balanced give and take, where knowledge is shared freely, without the constraints of hierarchy, allowing both mentor and mentee to grow from the interaction.

In the journey of growth and success, giving back stands as a pivotal moment, marking the completion of the support cycle in the entrepreneurial ecosystem. This generosity, whether through time, resources, or wisdom, is not just an act of duty but a rewarding opportunity to foster the growth of fellow entrepreneurs. It transforms the mentor-mentee dynamic, making it a mutual exchange that enriches both parties. By contributing to others' successes, we reinforce our collective interconnectedness and celebrate shared achievements. This culture of giving blurs the lines between helping and receiving, emphasizing the collective journey and triumphs in entrepreneurship.

## Celebrating Milestones and Successes

In the journey of building a business, key moments stand out, whether they're major milestones like securing a crucial deal, celebrating the anniversary of your business's launch, or hitting a specific sales goal. These milestones are more than just dates or numbers; they're shining markers highlighting how far you've come and pointing the way forward. Recognizing these accomplishments is crucial. It's a way to honor the hard work, dedication, and sometimes even the struggles that have gone into reaching these points. Celebrating these moments sincerely lifts morale and re-energizes everyone involved, giving fresh momentum to your business venture.

In the realm of relentless pursuit, where the horizon always stretches further, recognizing milestones becomes an act of reverence for the journey itself. It is an acknowledgment that every step forward, every hurdle crossed, reflects your resilience and determination. Such recognition can manifest in varied forms, from a quiet evening of reflection to an exuberant gathering of all who have been part of the journey. The mode of celebration, whether introspective or communal, matters less than the act itself, for in this pause lies the power to rekindle passion and reaffirm commitment.

Creating a culture of recognition within the company is essential for boosting team morale and motivation. This culture celebrates achievements, fostering a creative and enthusiastic environment. When team members see their efforts acknowledged, they are encouraged to fully commit and innovate. Celebratory events then become shared rituals that honor collective achievements and individual contributions, strengthening the team's bond and alignment with the company's mission.

In pursuing future goals, taking time to reflect acts as a pause, grounding us in the progress made and lessons learned. This reflective practice is like examining a map after a journey, revealing the distance traveled, the challenges faced, and unexpected paths that led to new insights. Rooted in past experiences, reflection illuminates the path ahead, offering clarity and direction. It can be personal, like meditation or journaling, or shared within the team through stories, each method providing a distinct perspective on the journey.

With the wisdom gained from reflection and the motivation from celebrated successes, planning for the future becomes a strategic and creative process. This planning, shaped by previous accomplishments and obstacles, forms the foundation for upcoming ventures. It's about setting goals and plotting the course to achieve them, considering any potential challenges, and creating plans to overcome or avoid them.

Though bold, this plan for the future is grounded in reality, leveraging past experiences to set objectives that are both visionary and realistic. It's a living document, constantly adapting as the business celebrates new successes and assimilates fresh insights, thereby keeping the business flexible, robust, and consistently inspired by a vision that extends far beyond the present.

Integrating these practices into your business journey creates a rich narrative that respects the past, cherishes the present, and looks forward to the future with excitement. This narrative is created from the vibrant colors of your achievements, the detailed lessons you've learned, and the shared experiences of your team. It stands as a tribute to the persistent spirit of entrepreneurship and the collaborative effort that defines your business.

# The Future of Entrepreneurship: Staying Ahead of the Curve

In a world where change is the only constant, entrepreneurs who stand still quickly recede into the background, overshadowed by those who move with purpose and foresight. The business landscape is ever-evolving, shaped by innovations and shifting consumer demands that wait for no one. To remain relevant and competitive, one must keep pace with industry trends and emerging technologies and anticipate them, acting not out of reaction but from a place of preparedness and strategic planning.

Navigating the future begins with keenly observing the present and identifying the faint signals amidst the noise that indicate emerging shifts in consumer behavior, technological advancements, and market dynamics. This vigilance involves a commitment to ongoing research, engaging with thought leaders and trendsetters, and analyzing data that reveal patterns and trajectories others might overlook. By embedding trend analysis into strategic planning, entrepreneurs can pivot their operations, marketing, and product development efforts to capitalize on upcoming shifts, ensuring they remain not just participants in their industry but leaders who shape its direction.

Maintaining a competitive edge hinges on innovation, daring to venture into uncharted territories with novel products, services, and operational models that challenge the status quo. This process is nurtured in a culture that values experimentation, where every outcome, be it a success or failure, is viewed as a learning opportunity. It's about being proactive by not just solving today's problems but also anticipating and creating solutions for future challenges. By adopting this mindset, businesses can stay ahead, ready with offerings that anticipate and exceed evolving consumer expectations.

As consumer awareness grows and the call for corporate responsibility becomes louder, integrating sustainable and ethical practices into the core of business operations is no longer optional but imperative. This integration speaks to a broader understanding of success that measures achievement not solely by profit margins but by the positive impact on society and the environment. Adopting sustainable practices, from sourcing materials responsibly to minimizing waste and reducing carbon footprints, reflects a commitment to stewardship that resonates with consumers and sets a business apart in a crowded marketplace. Moreover, it prepares the enterprise for a future where regulations around sustainability are likely to tighten, ensuring compliance and competitiveness in an eco-conscious world.

The entrepreneurship landscape is one of constant motion, where the only way to remain relevant is to move with purpose, guided by foresight, innovation, and a commitment to doing business in a way that benefits not just the individual but the world at large. As we close this chapter, we are reminded that the future of entrepreneurship is not a distant horizon to be reached but a path we pave with every decision. The future is ours to shape, with our choices today laying the foundation for a world where entrepreneurship continues to be a force for positive change.

# Chapter Eleven

# From Vision to Reality

This chapter provides a detailed guide through the essential final checks before your launch, offering a blueprint for this pivotal phase. It marks the intersection of legal considerations, operational readiness, marketing strategies, and personal preparation, each aspect vital for a seamless start.

## Finalizing Legal and Financial Structures

Setting up your business's legal and financial foundations is crucial, much like carefully arranging dominoes to ensure a successful cascade. This stage goes beyond just formalities; it's about establishing a robust framework to support your business's growth and protect against legal and financial risks. Key steps include registering your business, obtaining necessary licenses, and selecting the right business structure, each meticulously planned to set the stage for a triumphant launch.

## Operational Essentials

A successful launch fundamentally depends on the readiness of your operational systems, much like how a pilot meticulously checks every system before takeoff, from navigation to communication, ensuring everything functions perfectly. In this section, we focus on the operational heart of your business, including supply chain management, customer service protocols, and the strength of your technology infrastructure. Testing these systems goes beyond routine; it's a crucial assessment of your business's ability to efficiently and effectively meet market demands. Here, you will learn how to evaluate each operational aspect and discover strategies to enhance these systems, making sure they are not just operational but fine-tuned for peak performance.

## Marketing Launch Plan

Introducing your business to the world mirrors the excitement of an artist debuting their work at a gallery. It's the moment your hard work and creativity are showcased for public admiration. Think of your marketing launch plan as this grand opening, where your brand takes center stage, crafted to capture and hold your target audience's attention. This plan spans a wide array of marketing maneuvers, from drafting your inaugural press release and plotting your social media journey to initiating community events. Each content piece and interaction acts as a deliberate stroke in painting your brand's story, carefully designed to resonate with your audience and carve out a significant presence in the market from the get-go.

## Personal Preparedness

In the whirlwind of launching a business, the entrepreneur's well-being often takes a backseat. Yet, like an athlete before a race, your personal readiness, mental, physical, and emotional, is paramount to your performance. This segment delves into the often-overlooked aspect of launch preparation, emphasizing the importance of self-care, stress management, and maintaining a balanced perspective. It's a reminder that the strength of your business is intrinsically linked to your personal well-being, urging you to prioritize self-care amidst the demands of the launch. Practical tips for managing stress, maintaining physical health, and cultivating a mindset equipped to handle the challenges ahead are shared, ensuring you're prepared, resilient, and ready to navigate the highs and lows of entrepreneurship with grace and determination.

## Planning for the Future: Long-Term Goals and Strategies

In the realm of business, where uncertainty looms at every corner, and the market's whims can shift the ground beneath your feet, anchoring your venture to a solid foundation of long-term goals and strategies is not just prudent; it's a necessity. This forward-thinking mindset transcends mere survival, aiming instead for a legacy that stands the test of time.

Revisiting your business's vision and goals is essential. This isn't just about looking back; it's an active process of envisioning where your business could go. It means critically assessing if you're on the right path, keeping up with industry changes, and understanding how your personal goals have evolved through your entrepreneurial journey.

Strategic planning delineates your route toward long-term objectives. This meticulous process begins with the articulation of goals that resonate with your revised vision and challenge you to stretch beyond the comfort of familiarity. Identifying the resources, capital, talent, and technology necessary to guide you toward these goals is a critical next step. The heart of this strategic planning lies in outlining the steps to achieve your objectives, a sequence of ambitious and grounded actions, ensuring your venture remains agile yet focused, capable of weathering storms and capitalizing on favorable winds.

Businesses must employ risk management to navigate potential threats. This involves proactively identifying, evaluating, and mitigating risks that could derail your long-term goals. A comprehensive analysis of both internal and external factors, such as market fluctuations, regulatory shifts, and operational challenges, is critical. Developing contingency plans provides a safety net, allowing your business to remain adaptable and resilient in the face of unexpected challenges, ensuring you can adjust your course as needed.

Finally, the sustainability of your venture and its ability to thrive beyond the tenure of its current leadership hinges on effective succession planning. Succession planning speaks to the strength of your business model, culture, and vision, ensuring that the values and strategies that have defined your journey continue to guide the venture into the future. Whether through grooming internal candidates or identifying external successors, this process secures the continuity of your enterprise.

By tackling the intricacies of setting long-term goals and strategies, refining your business vision, engaging in strategic planning, managing risks, and planning for succession, your business is fortified against market uncertainties and poised for enduring success.

This chapter has equipped you with the knowledge to navigate current challenges and capitalize on future opportunities. Next, we transition from the broad planning and foresight required for long-term success to the nuances of daily operations, delving into tactical actions that maintain your business's agility and effectiveness in realizing its long-term ambitions.

> **Actions Step:** Use the Final Checklist to ensure all is prepared for the launch of your business.

# Conclusion

Hey there, fellow dreamer and soon-to-be entrepreneur. We've been on quite the journey together, haven't we? From that initial spark of an idea flickering in your mind to laying down the groundwork for making that dream a tangible reality, you've walked the path from a novice to a budding entrepreneur ready to take on the world. I hope you feel that shift within you, the confidence blooming with every page you've turned in this book.

We've unpacked a lot together, from understanding the pulse of your audience to piecing together a robust business plan that stands the test of time and scrutiny. We dove deep into the nuts and bolts of legal and financial foundations. And let's not forget the magic of marketing and branding, a realm where your business gets to show its true colors and connect with those it seeks to serve. Securing start-up capital wisely, maintaining your venture's financial health, and nailing those operational strategies aren't just chapters in a book; they're milestones in your entrepreneurial journey.

The stories and real-world examples shared weren't just to fill pages. They were there to show you that, yes, it's possible. Others have walked this path and found success, each story guiding you through your journey, illuminating the practical applications of everything we've discussed.

Now, I'm not just going to leave you with a pat on the back and a "good luck." No, I'm here to urge you to take that first step today if you haven't already. Entrepreneurship starts with a single step fueled by passion and a meticulously crafted plan. Yes, business ownership is a wild ride, filled with highs and lows, but it is rewarding. With persistence and the right strategies at your disposal, achieving your dreams is not just a possibility; it's within reach.

Remember, the road to success is rarely a straight line. It's a winding path filled with setbacks and challenges that will test you. But your adaptability and resilience will see you through these moments. Embrace them, learn from them, and come back stronger.

And just when you think you've "made it," remember, the entrepreneurial journey doesn't stop with the launch of your business. It's an ongoing adventure, a continuous path of growth, learning, and pivoting to meet new challenges head-on and seize the opportunities ahead.

Imagine, just for a moment, what the future could hold. A successful business, sure, but more than that, a legacy of impact, of making a difference in a way that only you can. It's not just a dream; it's a future that's waiting for you to make it happen.

So, here's my parting message to you: I believe in you. I believe in your ability to succeed and forge a path that others will look up to. You've got this, and I can't wait to see where your journey takes you.

And hey, when you do make it, don't forget to share your story. Share your challenges, triumphs, and lessons learned with the world. There's a community of like-minded souls out here eager to cheer you on, learn from you, and maybe, just maybe, be inspired to start their own journeys because of you.

Here's to your success, your future, and the incredible journey of entrepreneurship. Let's get out there and make some dreams a reality.

## Keeping the Game Alive

Now you have everything you need to start your own business and make your entrepreneurial dream a reality, it's time to pass on your newfound knowledge and show other readers where they can find the same help. Simply by leaving your honest opinion of this book on Amazon, you'll show other aspiring entrepreneurs where they can find the information they're looking for, and pass their passion for starting a business forward.

Thank you for your help. The spirit of entrepreneurship is kept alive when we pass on our knowledge – and you're helping us to do just that.

# References

Brex. (n.d.). [Title not specified]. Retrieved from https://www.brex.com/journal/start-up-budget

Built In. (n.d.). *7 tips to elevate your startup recruitment strategy.* Retrieved from https://builtin.com/recruiting/startup-recruitment

Business Development Bank of Canada. (n.d.). *How to make financial projections for a new business.* Retrieved from https://www.bdc.ca/en/articles-tools/start-buy-business/start-business/6-steps-making-financial-projections-new-business

Business News Daily. (n.d.). *How to conduct a market analysis for your business.* Retrieved from https://www.businessnewsdaily.com/15751-conduct-market-analysis.html

CA Expert Advisors. (n.d.). *Case studies of established companies that adapted and thrived.* Retrieved from https://www.caexpertadvisors.com/established-companies-case-studies-of-established-companies-that-adapted-and-thrived

Carta. (n.d.). *How to bootstrap your startup before raising a round.* Retrieved from https://carta.com/blog/bootstrapping/

CoverWallet. (n.d.). *7 tips for small business supply chain management.* Retrieved from https://www.coverwallet.com/business-tips/supply-chain-management

crowdSPRING. (n.d.). *35 legal mistakes every startup and growing business must avoid.* Retrieved from https://www.crowdspring.com/blog/legal-mistakes/

Dacosta, C. (2019, January 31). *3 reasons why brand storytelling is the future of marketing.* Forbes. Retrieved from https://www.forbes.com/sites/celinnedacosta/2019/01/31/3-reasons-why-brand-storytelling-is-the-future-of-marketing/

DigitalOcean. (n.d.). *The complete guide to content marketing for startups.* Retrieved from https://www.digitalocean.com/resources/article/content-marketing-for-startups

Dividend.com. (n.d.). *14 failed businesses from successful entrepreneurs*. Retrieved from https://www.dividend.com/how-to-invest/14-failed-businesses-from-wildly-successful-billionaires/

Failory. (2024). *Startup branding: What is it & how to do it in 2024*. Retrieved from https://www.failory.com/blog/startup-branding

FinancesOnline. (2024). *16 entrepreneurship trends for 2024: New forecasts & a....* Retrieved from https://financesonline.com/entrepreneurship-trends/

Fit Small Business. (n.d.). *25 best home office setup ideas (+ productivity hacks)*. Retrieved from https://fitsmallbusiness.com/home-office-setup/

Forbes. (2023, August 7). *Scaling your business: Strategies for achieving rapid business growth*. Retrieved from https://www.forbes.com/sites/forbesbusinesscouncil/2023/08/07/scaling-your-business-strategies-for-achieving-rapid-business-growth/

Forbes Advisor. (n.d.). [Title not specified]. Retrieved from https://www.forbes.com/advisor/business/customer-retention-strategies/

Google for Small Business. (n.d.). *SEO basics: 5 tips & best practices*. Retrieved from https://smallbusiness.withgoogle.com/free-google-training/what-is-seo/

Harvard Business Review. (2018, May). *Strategy for start-ups*. Retrieved from https://hbr.org/2018/05/strategy-for-start-ups

HeroX. (n.d.). *10 ways to foster innovation in your company*. Retrieved from https://www.herox.com/blog/1063-10-ways-to-foster-innovation-in-your-company

Hiver. (n.d.). *How to create a successful customer loyalty program*. Retrieved from https://hiverhq.com/blog/customer-loyalty-program

HubSpot. (n.d.). *How to conduct market research for startups*. Retrieved from https://www.hubspot.com/startups/resources/market-research-for-startups

HubSpot Blog. (n.d.). *The most effective types of content on social media*. Retrieved from https://blog.hubspot.com/sales/sales-strategy

HubSpot Blog. (2024). *50 small business marketing ideas for 2024*. Retrieved from https://blog.hubspot.com/marketing/small-business-marketing-guide

Indiegogo. (2023). *Top 10 crowdfunding campaigns of 2023 so far*. Retrieved from https://go.indiegogo.com/blog/2023/08/top-10-crowdfunding-campaigns-of-2023-so-far.html

Inviqa. (n.d.). *A guide to cross-border tax in the EU, USA, and Australia*. Retrieved from https://inviqa.com/blog/pocket-guide-cross-border-tax-eu-usa-and-australia

LaunchX. (n.d.). *How to form a startup legal entity*. Retrieved from https://www.launchx.com/command-post/articles/how-to-form-a-startup-legal-entity

LinkedIn. (2024). *SEO for startups: A guide to grow your business in 2024*. Retrieved from https://www.linkedin.com/pulse/8-effective-sales-strategies-startups-entrepreneurs

MasterClass. (n.d.). *Guide to pitch decks: 10 elements to include in a pitch deck*. Retrieved from https://www.masterclass.com/articles/pitch-deck-guide

MasterClass. (2024). *How to create a customer persona: 2024 step-by-step guide*. Retrieved from https://www.masterclass.com/articles/unique-value-proposition-guide

McKinsey & Company. (n.d.). *A better way to build a brand: The community flywheel*. Retrieved from https://www.mckinsey.com/capabilities/growth-marketing-and-sales/our-insights/a-better-way-to-build-a-brand-the-community-flywheel

NerdWallet. (n.d.). [Title not specified]. Retrieved from https://www.nerdwallet.com/article/small-business/business-entity

Oregon Small Business Development Center Network. (n.d.). *Tips on how to expand your small business internationally*. Retrieved from https://oregonsbdc.org/tips-on-how-to-expand-your-small-business-internationally/

ProjectionHub. (n.d.). *How to forecast revenue for a startup | Read our 12 tips*. Retrieved from https://blog.projectionhub.com/12-steps-to-create-revenue-projections-for-any-startup/

SCORE.org. (n.d.). *10 tech tools for small businesses*. Retrieved from https://www.score.org/resource/blog-post/10-tech-tools-small-businesses

SentiSum. (n.d.). *Customer feedback analysis: Step-by-step + template*. Retrieved from https://www.sentisum.com/customer-feedback-analysis

Shopify. (n.d.). *21 time management tips for entrepreneurs*. Retrieved from https://www.shopify.com/blog/120436229-time-management-tips

Shopify. (n.d.). *What is product development? 7 steps to making a....* Retrieved from https://www.shopify.com/blog/product-development-process

Starbucks Corporation. (2021). *Annual report 2021*. Retrieved from Starbucks Investors Relations

Stevens & Tate Marketing. (n.d.). *5 SMART goal examples for business development*. Retrieved from https://stevens-tate.com/articles/5-smart-goal-examples/

Taylor, B. (2014). *How Starbucks is using its coffee clout to roast the competition*. Fortune Magazine. Retrieved from Fortune.com

U.S. Chamber of Commerce. (n.d.). *Accounting basics every new business owner should learn*. Retrieved from https://www.uschamber.com/co/run/finance/basic-accounting-skills-small-business

U.S. News & World Report. (2023). *Best small business accounting software of 2023*. Retrieved from https://www.usnews.com/360-reviews/business/best-small-business-accounting-software

U.S. Small Business Administration. (n.d.). *Choose your business name*. Retrieved from https://www.sba.gov/business-guide/launch-your-business/choose-your-business-name

U.S. Small Business Administration. (n.d.). *Write your business plan*. Retrieved from https://www.sba.gov/business-guide/plan-your-business/write-your-business-plan

Vengreso. (n.d.). *Pitching to angel investors: Strategies for success and growth*. Retrieved from https://vengreso.com/blog/pitching-angel-investors

Wikipedia contributors. (n.d.). *List of legal entity types by country*. In Wikipedia, The Free Encyclopedia. Retrieved from https://en.wikipedia.org/wiki/List_of_legal_entity_types_by_country